TSI TEXAS SUCCESS INITIATIVE
READING & WRITING STUDY GUIDE
ADVANTAGE+ EDITION

TSI Texas Success Initiative Reading and Writing Study Guide Advantage Plus Edition

TABLE OF CONTENTS

REFERENCES:

The literary texts in this publication have been reproduced from the following sources:

The Yellow Wallpaper by Charlotte Perkins Gilman (Reading Test 1, Literary Text 1)

Robinson Crusoe by Daniel Defoe (Reading Test 1, Literary Text 2)

A Story of the Days to Come by HG Wells (Reading Test 2, Literary Text 1)

Oliver Twist by Charles Dickens (Reading Test 2, Literary Text 2)

The Woman in White by Wilkie Collins (Reading Test 3, Literary Text 1)

Tess of the D'Ubervilles by Thomas Hardy (Reading Test 3, Literary Text 2)

The texts used in the reading passage comparison section have been reproduced under Private Label Rights.

TSI READING PRACTICE TEST 1

Read the passage and then select the correct answer to the question. You need to answer based on ideas that are stated, suggested, or implied in the passage.

1. Research shows that the recent rise in teenage smoking has primarily taken place in youth from more affluent families, whose parents are both working. Therefore, these teenagers are not from disadvantaged homes, as most people seem to believe. The facts demonstrate quite the opposite because the most striking and precipitous rise in smoking has been for teenagers from the most financially advantageous backgrounds.

   What is the primary purpose of this passage?
   A.   to provide information on a recent trend
   B.   to emphasize the dangers of smoking
   C.   to dispel a common misconception ✓
   D.   to highlight the difference between two types of teenagers

2. Gene splicing, the process whereby a small part of the DNA of one organism is removed and inserted into the DNA chain of another organism, has produced results like the super tomato. In order to create the super tomato, the gene resistant to cold temperatures on the DNA chain of a particular type of cold-water fish was isolated, removed, and inserted into an ordinary tomato plant. This resulted in a new type of tomato plant that can thrive in cold weather conditions.

   From this passage, it seems safe to conclude that
   A.   the super tomato was the first case of gene splicing. ✓
   B.   the super tomato is only one example of gene splicing.
   C.   DNA from tomatoes has also been inserted into certain types of fish.
   D.   many people object to gene splicing.

3. In 1804, Meriwether Lewis and William Clark began an expedition across the western United States, then known as the Louisiana Territory. The two men had met years earlier and established a long-lasting friendship. When Lewis was later a young captain in the army, he received a letter from President Thomas Jefferson offering him funding to explore the western country. With Jefferson's permission, Lewis offered a partnership in the expedition to his friend Clark. When their journey had safely concluded 8,000 miles later, President Jefferson purchased the Louisiana Territory for fifteen million dollars.

   The purpose of the passage is
   A.   to give the background to Lewis and Clark's westward expedition.
   B.   to defend the purchase of the Louisiana Territory.
   C.   to state a crucial decision made by Thomas Jefferson.
   D.   to compare the skills of Lewis and Clark.

4. The Watergate burglary had many aspects, but at its center was President Richard Nixon. Throughout the investigation of the burglary, government officials denied involvement in the crime. An extensive cover-up operation followed in an attempt to conceal those who were involved in planning the break-in. Yet, this subterfuge failed when the FBI investigated the one-hundred-dollar bills that were found in the pockets of the burglars. After making inquiries, the FBI discovered that this money originated from the Committee for the Re-election of the President, thereby confirming governmental involvement. In the end, individuals who had entered the highest branches of the American government to serve and protect the people went to prison instead.

What is main reason why the cover-up of the Watergate break-in failed?
A.   because the Committee for the Re-election of the President denied involvement
B.   because of the subterfuge of the FBI
C.   because the burglars' money was traced back to a governmental organization ✓
D.   because its ringleaders went to prison

5. Highly concentrated radioactive waste is lethal and can remain so for thousands of years. Accordingly, the disposal of this material remains an issue in most energy-producing countries around the world. In the United States, for example, liquid forms of radioactive waste are usually stored in stainless steel tanks. For extra protection, the tanks are double-walled and surrounded by a concrete covering that is one meter thick. This storage solution is also utilized the United Kingdom, in most cases. The long term problem lies in the fact that nuclear waste generates heat as the radioactive atoms decay. This excess heat could ultimately result in a radioactive leak. Therefore, the liquid needs to be cooled by pumping cold water into coils inside the tanks. Of course, this means that the tanks are only a temporary storage solution. The answer to the long term storage of nuclear waste may be fusing the waste into glass cylinders that are stored deep underground.

Which of the following assumptions has most influenced the writer? D
A.   The threat of a radioactive leak is exaggerated by the public.
B.   The storage of radioactive waste in stainless steel tanks is extremely dangerous.
C.   The United Kingdom normally follows practices that the United States has adopted.
D.   A radioactive leak would have disastrous consequences around the globe.

6. Cancer occurs when cells in the body begin to divide abnormally and form more cells without control or order. There are some factors which are known to increase the risk of cancer. Smoking is the largest single cause of death from cancer in the United States. In addition, poor food choices increase cancer risk. Indeed, research shows that there is a definite link between the consumption of high-fat food and cancer.

   From this passage, we can infer that *A* → *Say Link*
   - A.   a low-fat diet can reduce the risk of cancer.
   - B.   smoking usually causes cells to divide abnormally. *50/50*
   - C.   the consumption of high-fat food has increased in recent years. ✗
   - D.   most cancer sufferers have made poor food choices.

7. The theory of multiple intelligence (MI) is rapidly replacing the intelligence quotient, or IQ. The IQ, long considered the only valid way of measuring intelligence, has come under criticism because it inheres in many cultural biases. For this reason, there has been a movement away from the IQ test, which is now seen as an indication of a person's academic ability. On the other hand, multiple intelligence measures practical skills such as spatial, visual, and musical ability.

   The main idea of the passage is that *C*
   - A.   there are cultural biases in the IQ test.
   - B.   the IQ does not take visual or spatial ability into account.
   - C.   the theory of multiple intelligence is superior to the concept of IQ.
   - D.   multiple intelligence is a measure of an individual's practical abilities.

8. Around the world today, more than a billion people still do not have fresh, clean drinking water available on a daily basis. Hundreds of thousands of people in developing countries die needlessly every year because of the consumption of unclean, disease-ridden water. Simply stated, fresh water saves lives. However, what has been understood only recently is that the provision for fresh water around the globe also protects the environment because it means that those who manage water supplies must evaluate in more detail why and how developed countries consume and pollute their available water. Without this evaluation, an ever-increasing number of individuals will continue to die from water-related diseases.

   We can conclude from the information in this passage that
   - A.   water-related disease will decline in the future.
   - B.   water-related deaths could be avoided. ✓
   - C.   children are the most vulnerable to water-related disease and death.
   - D.   developed countries manage their water supplies better than developing countries.

9. Sir Isaac Newton had the prescience to appreciate that his study of natural phenomena was of great import for the scientific community and for society as a whole. It is because of Newton's work that we currently understand the effect of gravity on the earth as a global system. As a result of Newton's investigation into the subject of gravity, we know today that geological features such as mountains and canyons can cause variances in the Earth's gravitational force. Newton must also be acknowledged for the realization that the force of gravity becomes less robust as the distance from the equator diminishes, due to the rotation of the earth, as well as the declining mass and density of the planet from the equator to the poles.

What is the author's main purpose?
A. to analyze natural phenomena
B. to reconcile various gravitational theories
C. to identify a reservation which Newton experienced
D. to emphasize the significance of Newton's achievement ✓

10. The corpus of research on Antarctica has resulted in an abundance of factual data. For example, we now know that more than ninety nine percent of the land is completely covered by snow and ice, making Antarctica the coldest continent on the planet. This inhospitable climate has brought about the adaptation of a plethora of plants and biological organisms present on the continent. An investigation into the sedimentary geological formations provides testimony to the process of adaptation. Sediments recovered from the bottom of Antarctic lakes, as well as bacteria discovered in ice, have revealed the history of climate change over the past 10,000 years.

According to the passage, the plants and organisms in Antarctica
A. have survived because of the process of adaptation. ✓
B. are the result of sedimentary geological formations.
C. cover more than 99% of the land surface.
D. grow in the bottom of lakes on the continent.

Read Passages 1 and 2 below. Then answer the questions. You need to answer based on ideas that are stated, suggested, or implied in the passage.

Passage 1:

Hamlet said: "We end the heartache, and the thousand natural shocks that flesh is heir to." It has always been the function of the actor to be the emotional physician, who gives solace, encouragement and freedom of feeling to people who need it – when they need it.

Acting is a challenging profession, and this has been the challenge of the actor since the beginning of time. He or she is the torchbearer of a great tradition – a fearless trail blazer into an expanding frontier. Actors must not be afraid to be the catalyst between progress and people. They must approach their calling with authority, humility, and fearlessness.

As the human race progressed, instinct gave way to inspiration. Inspiration became a creative tool of civilization. To be aware of creation, which is born of inspiration, and to be able to direct that creation, are the result of intelligence.

Accordingly, the duty of the serious actor is great. In ancient Greece thousands of years ago, acting served the same purpose that it still serves today. Its fundamental purpose has not changed from the time cave men lined up in a circle and performed their ritualistic chants and pantomimic dances to stir the emotions of their audience. Through these rituals, which were basically acts, the primitive emotions were excited to a point of emotional stimulation that propelled our civilization onward.

Passage 2:

There has been a fundamental change in the relationship between the actor and the audience in recent years. According to Aristotelian principles, actors should provoke an emotional catharsis in the members of the audience. Traditionally, actors have provided this emotional release, but this is far from the case in many modern motion pictures and television programs. Many performances and productions nowadays lack gravitas; rather, they are based on contrived stories or weak plots that have been created merely as mindless diversions. When actors engage in such vacuous performances, they do not even begin to serve the higher purpose of their profession.

11. How would the writer of Passage 1 respond to the last sentence of Passage 2? (When actors . . . profession.)
    A. by pointing out that actors sometimes fail to exemplify Aristotelian principles.
    B. by asserting that these performances do serve a purpose because they give the audience the opportunity to experience "freedom of feeling."

C.   by claiming that productions do not always help audience members to overcome emotional tensions.

D.   by arguing that the primary role of the actor is to entertain the audience.

12.   The writer of Passage 2 would most likely criticize the writer of Passage 1 for

A.   comparing actors to Hamlet. *D*

B.   providing the example of acting in ancient Greece.

C.   claiming that inspiration is the "creative tool of civilization."

D.   stating that acting has "propelled our civilization onward."

13.   Both passages suggest that *A*

A.   acting is a challenging profession.

B.   modern acting has evolved to a higher level from traditional acting.

C.   actors often fail to provoke an emotional response from the audience.

D.   actors need to be intelligent in order to perform well.

Read Passages 1 and 2 below. Then answer the questions. You need to answer based on ideas that are stated, suggested, or implied in the passage.

Passage 1:

Credit card debt is a major cause of over one million bankruptcies each year. The reason is that many people get a credit card without researching and reading the fine print. By the time annual fees are added on, along with spending indiscriminately, payments are missed, which causes balances to skyrocket.

Although we all like to place the blame on the credit cards and the credit card companies, individuals themselves are the real culprits. In short, if your credit card spending is out of control, you need to keep in mind that the real cause of your financial mess is you.

If you can summon enough willpower and strength to manage your finances and spending, then you will find yourself the winner in the game of finance. It may be easy to get into debt, but getting out of debt is much more difficult.

One simple phrase can sum up the solution to financial problems. If you don't have the money to spend, then don't spend it!

Passage 2:

It has to be said that external forces and market conditions have a huge impact on personal financial situations. Have you ever noticed that the things you buy at the store go up a few pennies between shopping trips? Not every week and not by much – just little by little – but they continue to creep up.

But there is a way that the effect of price increases upon personal finances can be minimized: buy in quantity when prices are low. My philosophy is to set out to find the best prices I can get on quantity purchases of such things as bathroom items and dry and canned food, even if I have to use my credit card to get them. You will be surprised by how much you can save, for example, by buying a twenty pound bag of rice as opposed to a one pound bag.

14. The writer of Passage 1 would disagree most strongly with which of the following statements from Passage 2? A/ C
    A. External forces and market conditions have a huge impact on personal financial situations.
    B. The things you buy at the store go up a few pennies between shopping trips.

C. But there is a way that the effect of price increases upon personal finances can be minimized: buy in quantity when prices are low.

D. My philosophy is to set out to find the best prices I can get on quantity purchases of such things as bathroom items and dry and canned food, even if I have to use my credit card to get them.

15. How would the writer of Passage 2 most likely respond to the assertion of the writer of Passage 1 that "the real cause of your financial mess is you"? *B*

A. You can take control of your spending by making bulk purchases.

B Market conditions can have a real effect on personal finances. The individual is not always to blame.

C. Sometimes you have to spend in order to save.

D. Credit cards help shoppers to save money in the long run.

Read the passage and then select the correct answers to the questions. You need to answer based on ideas that are stated, suggested, or implied in the passage.

LITERARY TEXT 1

One of those sprawling flamboyant patterns committing every artistic sin. It is dull enough to confuse the eye in following, pronounced enough to constantly irritate and provoke study, and when you follow the lame uncertain curves for a little distance they suddenly commit suicide—plunge off at outrageous angles, destroy themselves in unheard of contradictions.

The color is repellent, almost revolting; a smoldering unclean yellow, strangely faded by the slow-turning sunlight. It is a dull yet lurid orange in some places, a sickly sulfur tint in others. No wonder the children hated it! I should hate it myself if I had to live in this room long.

These nervous troubles are dreadfully depressing. John does not know how much I really suffer. He knows there is no REASON to suffer, and that satisfies him. Of course it is only nervousness. It does weigh on me so not to do my duty in any way!

I meant to be such a help to John, such a real rest and comfort, and here I am a comparative burden already!

Nobody would believe what an effort it is to do what little I am able,—to dress and entertain, and other things. It is fortunate Mary is so good with the baby. Such a dear baby! And yet I CANNOT be with him, it makes me so nervous.

I suppose John never was nervous in his life. He laughs at me so about this wall-paper! At first he meant to repaper the room, but afterwards he said that I was letting it get the better of me, and that nothing was worse for a nervous patient than to give way to such fancies.

He said that after the wall-paper was changed it would be the heavy bedstead, and then the barred windows, and then that gate at the head of the stairs, and so on.

"You know the place is doing you good," he said, "and really, dear, I don't care to renovate the house just for a three months' rental."

I wish I could get well faster. But I must not think about that. This paper looks to me as if it KNEW what a vicious influence it had!

16.   When the narrator uses the word "it" in paragraph 1, she is referring to
     A.   the room.
     B.   the baby.

C. the wallpaper. ✓
D. the heavy bedstead.

17. Why does the narrator use capitalization in this sentence?: "He knows there is no REASON to suffer, and that satisfies him. Of course it is only nervousness."
   A. She wants to imply that her husband thinks that she is irrational. *A*
   B. She is trying to point out the gravity of her situation.
   C. She wants to suggest that men are more reasonable than women.
   D. She is praising her husband for being logical.

18. This passage implies that the relationship between the narrator and her husband is *B*
   A. contented.
   B. strained.
   C. resigned.
   D. violent.

19. From this passage, we can infer that the narrator *C*
   A. is a poor mother.
   B. regrets her marriage.
   C. is suffering from mental illness.
   D. could be dangerous to society.

20. When the narrator uses the phrase "such fancies" in paragraph 6, she is referring to *D*
   A. having Mary take care of the baby.
   B. being so nervous about her situation.
   C. her husband's refusal to renovate the entire house for her.
   D. her husband's opinion about her desire to put up new wallpaper.

Read the passage and then select the correct answers to the questions. You need to answer based on ideas that are stated, suggested, or implied in the passage.

LITERARY TEXT 2

I cannot say that after this, for five years, any extraordinary thing happened to me, but I lived on in the same course, in the same posture and place.

At last, being eager to view the circumference of my little kingdom, I resolved upon my cruise; and accordingly I victualed my ship for the voyage, putting in two dozen of loaves (cakes I should call them) of barley-bread, an earthen pot full of parched rice (a food I ate a good deal of), a little bottle of rum, half a goat, and powder and shot for killing more, and two large watch-coats, of those which, as I mentioned before, I had saved out of the seamen's chests; these I took, one to lie upon, and the other to cover me in the night.

It was the 6th of November, in the sixth year of my reign - or my captivity, which you please - that I set out on this voyage, and I found it much longer than I expected; having secured my boat, I took my gun and went on shore, climbing up a hill, which seemed to overlook that point where I saw the full extent of it, and resolved to venture. In my viewing the sea from that hill where I stood, I perceived a strong, and indeed a most furious current.

And now I saw how easy it was for the providence of God to make even the most miserable condition of mankind worse. Now I looked back upon my former abode as the most pleasant place in the world and all the happiness my heart could wish for was to be but there again. I stretched out my hands to it, with eager wishes - "O happy desert!" said I, "I shall never see thee more. O miserable creature! whither am going?" Then I reproached myself with my unthankful temper, and that I had repined at my solitary condition; and now what would I give to be on shore there again! Thus, we never see the true state of our condition till it is illustrated to us by its contraries, nor know how to value what we enjoy, but by the want of it.

21. From the descriptions provided in the passage, the reader can understand that the narrator is describing his life
     A. as a sailor.
     B. on a deserted island. ✓
     C. while being stranded in the desert.
     D. on a cruise ship.

22. What does the narrator mean when he says that he "victualed" the ship for the voyage?
    A. He loaded hunting supplies.
    B. He packed clothing for the voyage.
    C. He put on food and edible supplies. ✓
    D. He checked that he had bed clothes.

23. What is the narrator's tone when he states: "It was the 6th of November, in the sixth year of my reign"?
    A. sarcastic ✓
    B. mournful
    C. factual
    D. sincere

24. What is the best paraphrase of the following sentence from the last paragraph of the passage: "Then I reproached myself with my unthankful temper, and that I had repined at my solitary condition; and now what would I give to be on shore there again!"
    A. I told myself off for being ungrateful about my previous plight.
    B. I considered the bounty to which I had had access, and I regretted that I had felt lonely.
    C. I beat myself up having been ungrateful about being alone because I longed to return to where I was before.
    D. I scolded myself for not appreciating all that I had had before my voyage and for having felt lonely because now I wished that I could go back there again. ✓

25. What can we infer when the narrator states: "we never see the true state of our condition till it is illustrated to us by its contraries"?
    A. He misses the life he had before embarking on his journey. ✓
    B. He wishes he could be a more grateful person.
    C. He thinks that others could learn a lesson from his experiences.
    D. We learn who we really are when we feel contrary to others.

TSI PRACTICE TEST 1 – ANSWERS AND EXPLANATIONS

1. The correct answer is C. Misconception means misunderstanding. The phrase "as most people seem to believe" in the passage indicates that there has been a misunderstanding. The passage also provides information on a trend, but the primary purpose is to clear up a misunderstanding.

2. The correct answer is B. The phrase "results like the super tomato" indicates that the super tomato is only one example. The other ideas are not implied by the passage.

3. The correct answer is A. The passage describes how Lewis and Clark met and why they made their famous expedition together. The passage mentions Thomas Jefferson, but this is only a minor point of the passage. The passage does not defend the purchase, nor does it make any comparisons.

4. The correct answer is C. The key sentence is: "After making inquiries, the FBI discovered that this money originated from the Committee for the Re-election of the President, thereby confirming governmental involvement." This sentence signals the reason why the break in failed when it uses the word "thereby." Answers A and D are mentioned in the passage, but they are not the reason for the failure. Answer B is not stated in the passage. Note that the subterfuge was part of the cover-up, not an action by the FBI.

5. The correct answer is D. The author implies that a radioactive leak would have dire consequences since he opens the passage with this sentence: "Highly concentrated radioactive waste is lethal and can remain so for thousands of years."

6. The correct answer is A. The passage states: "Indeed, research shows that there is a definite link between the consumption of high-fat food and cancer." So, conversely, we can understand that a low-fat diet will decrease the chances of getting cancer. The other answers are not implied in the passage.

7. The correct answer is C. The passage states that MI "is rapidly replacing . . . IQ." It also states that the IQ test "has come under criticism recently." Therefore, answer C gives the main idea. Answers A, B, and D are specific points from the passage.

8. The correct answer is B. The passage uses the phrases "people . . . die needlessly" and "fresh water saves lives." Therefore, it is the writer's viewpoint that the deaths could be avoided. The information in answers A, C, and D is not stated in the passage.

9. The correct answer is D. The passage uses the word "prescience," which means insight, to describe Newton in the topic sentence. Later, the writer uses the phrases "because of Newton's work . . . we currently understand" and "As a result of Newton's investigation . . . we know today." Therefore, the writer believes that Newton made a significant achievement.

10. The correct answer is A. The passage states: "This inhospitable climate has brought about the adaptation . . . "

11. The correct answer is B. The first paragraph of passage 1 states that a function of the actor is to give "freedom of feeling to people who need it – when they need it." The author of passage 1 would argue that even below-par performances, such as those described in passage 2, achieve this purpose.

12. The correct answer is D. The author of passage 2 states: "Many performances and productions nowadays lack gravitas." A lack of gravitas means that performances do not have a serious purpose. Propelling a civilization onward is an extremely serious purpose, so the author of passage 2 would certainly disagree with this statement.

13. The correct answer is A. The author of passage 1 states in paragraph 2 that "acting is a challenging profession." The author of passage 2 implies that acting is challenging because he talks about recent changes in the acting profession, as well as the fact that acting should serve a higher purpose.

14. The correct answer is D. The writer of passage 1 speaks out against credit card debt, so she would disagree with the following statement from passage 2: "My philosophy is to set out to find the best prices I can get on quantity purchases of such things as bathroom items and dry and canned food, even if I have to use my credit card to get them."

15. The correct answer is B. The writer of passage 2 would disagree with the statement that "the real cause of your financial mess is you" because she asserts that "external forces and market conditions have a huge impact on personal financial situations."

16. The correct answer is C. We know that the narrator is talking about the wallpaper because she is describing the patterns on the paper. She then goes on to talk about the wallpaper in the majority of the passage.

17. The correct answer is A. For emphasis questions like this one, think about how the statement would sound if spoken aloud. The word "reason" would be emphasized if the narrator were speaking in a sarcastic way. The narrator also talks about the way in which the conclusion that she is not being reasonable satisfies her husband. She is talking about the situation from his point of view, not hers, so she is implying that he thinks she is irrational.

18. The correct answer is B. The passage mentions various ways in which the narrator's husband will not accommodate her wishes, so the reader can assume that their relationship is difficult or strained.

19. The correct answer is C. The narrator speaks about nervousness, which is a euphemism for nervous breakdown or depression. She states at the beginning of paragraph 3: "These nervous troubles are dreadfully depressing."

20. The correct answer is D. Her husband's opinion is that it is fanciful or whimsical to put up new wallpaper for a short-term lease.

21. The correct answer is B. The narrator talks about a ship, his captivity, and being in an isolated condition, so we can surmise that he is stranded on a deserted island.

22. The correct answer is C. "Victual" is an antiquated word meaning food. We can understand this from the context of the passage because the narrator talks about putting bread, rice, and meat on the ship.

23. The correct answer is A. The narrator is being sarcastic. He is stranded and alone, so there is no one over whom he can reign.

24. The correct answer is D. "Reproach" means scold; "unthankful temper" means not appreciating what one has; "solitary condition" means loneliness, and the utterance "what I would give to be on shore there again" means that he wants to go back to the island.

25. The correct answer is A. The statement "we never see the true state of our condition till it is illustrated to us by its contraries" would be expressed in present-day English as "you don't know what you've got until it's gone."

TSI WRITING PRACTICE TEST 1

Read the draft essay below and then choose the best answers to the questions that follow.

(**1**) A group of English separatists known as the Pilgrims left England. (**2**) When they left England, they went to live in Amsterdam in 1608. (**3**) After spending a few years in their new city however many members of the group felt that they did not have enough independence. (**4**) In 1617, the Pilgrims decided to leave Amsterdam to immigrate to America.

(**5**) Due to their lack of social standing, they had many financial problems that prevented them from beginning the journey. (**6**) Their inability to finance themselves caused many disputes and disagreements. (**7**) The Pilgrims finally managed to resolve these conflicts when they obtained financing from a well-known and respected London businessman named Thomas Weston.

(**8**) Having secured Weston's monetary support, the group returned to England to pick up some additional passengers. (**9**) After 65 days at sea, the Pilgrims reached America in December 1620. (**10**) The early days of their new lives were filled with hope and promise. (**11**) The harsh winter proved to be too much for some of the settlers. (**12**) Nearly half of the Pilgrims died during that first winter.

1. What is the best way to revise and combine sentences 1 and 2?

   A. A group of English separatists known as the Pilgrims went to live in Amsterdam in 1608 after they left England.
   B. A group of English separatists known as the Pilgrims left England and went to live in Amsterdam in 1608.
   C. A group of English separatists known as the Pilgrims left England, they went to live in Amsterdam in 1608.
   D. A group of English separatists known as the Pilgrims left England since they went to live in Amsterdam in 1608.

2.   What is the best revision to sentence 3? Sentence 3 is provided again here for ease of reference.

After spending a few years in their new city however many members of the group felt that they did not have enough independence.

A.   Put commas after the word "city" and after the word "however."
B.   Replace the words "did not" with the contraction "didn't."
C.   Place a comma after the word "years."
D.   Replace the word "spending" with the words "they spent."

3.   Which one of the following words or phrases would be best inserted at the beginning of sentence 4?

A   However,
B.   In addition,
C.   Therefore,
D.   Surprisingly,

4.   Where is the best place to insert the following sentence?

Most of the separatists were poor farmers who did not have much education or social status.

A.   Before sentence 2
B.   Before sentence 3
C.   Before sentence 4
D.   Before sentence 5

5.   Which of the following is the best revision to sentence 5? Sentence 5 is provided again here for ease of reference.

Due to their lack of social standing, they had many financial problems that prevented them from beginning the journey.

A.   Place the phrase "it was said that" before "they."
B.   Replace the word "they" with the words "the group."
C.   Delete the phrase "the journey."
D.   Replace the word "financial" with "economic."

6.   What is the best way to revise and combine sentences 6 and 7?

    A.   Their inability to finance themselves caused many disputes and disagreements; the Pilgrims finally managed to resolve these conflicts when they obtained financing from a well-known and respected London businessman named Thomas Weston.

    B.   The Pilgrims finally managed to resolve their conflicts when they obtained financing from a well-known and respected London businessman named Thomas Weston, although their inability to finance themselves had caused many disputes and disagreements.

    C.   Even though their inability to finance themselves caused many disputes and disagreements, the Pilgrims managed to resolve these conflicts when they obtained financing from a well-known and respected London businessman named Thomas Weston.

    D.   Their inability to finance themselves caused many disputes and disagreements, nevertheless, the Pilgrims finally managed to resolve these conflicts when they obtained financing from a well-known and respected London businessman named Thomas Weston.

7.   Which of the following sentences would be best inserted between sentences 8 and 9?

    A.   New evidence indicates that the Pilgrims suffered from many diseases that would have been treatable had they had access to modern-day antibiotics.

    B.   Some scholars argue that life on the *Mayflower* was filled with contention and in-fighting.

    C.   The life of Pocahontas followed a completely different trajectory.

    D.   They boarded a large ship called the *Mayflower* on September 16, 1620.

8.   Where is the best place to insert the following sentence?

Plymouth, a town about 35 miles southeast of Boston in the New England state of Massachusetts, was established by the Pilgrims once they had settled in America.

    A.   After sentence 9
    B.   After sentence 10
    C.   After sentence 11
    D.   After sentence 12

9. What is the best way to combine and revise sentences 10 and 11?

    A.   The harsh winter proved to be too much for some of the settlers, while the early days of their new lives were filled with hope and promise.

    B.   The harsh winter proved to be too much for some of the settlers, whereas the early days of their new lives were filled with hope and promise.

    C.   The early days of their new lives were filled with hope and promise because later the harsh winter proved to be too much for some of the settlers.

    D.   While the early days of their new lives were filled with hope and promise, the harsh winter proved to be too much for some of the settlers.

10.   Which one of the following words or phrases would be best inserted at the beginning of sentence 12? Sentence 12 is provided again here for ease of reference.

Nearly half of the Pilgrims died during that first winter

    A.   Ironically,
    B.   Unfortunately,
    C.   Finally,
    D.   To conclude,

Select the best substitute for the underlined parts of the following ten sentences. The first answer [choice A] is identical to the original sentence. If you think the original sentence is best, then choose A as your answer.

11.   Although she was only sixteen years old, <u>the university accepted her application because of her outstanding grades</u>.

    A.   the university accepted her application because of her outstanding grades.

    B.   her application was accepted by the university because of her outstanding grades.

    C   her outstanding grades resulted in her application being accepted by the university.

    D.   she was accepted to study at the university after applying because of her outstanding grades.

12.   Never in my life <u>have I seen such a beautiful sight.</u>
    A.   have I seen such a beautiful sight.
    B.   I have seen such a beautiful sight
    C.   such a beautiful sight I have seen.
    D.   such a beautiful sight I saw.

13. After the loss of a loved one, the bereaved can experience shock, numbness, and they also get depressed.
   A. shock, numbness, and they also get depressed.
   B. shock, numbness, and depression.
   C. shock, numbness, and get depressed.
   D. shock, numbness, and depressed.

14. I was going to study this evening, however the noise next door made it impossible.
   A. evening, however the noise next door
   B. evening: however the noise next door
   C. evening, however, the noise next door
   D. evening. However, the noise next door

15. She was hoping to buy a new car which would be spacious enough to transport her equipment.
   A. a new car which would be spacious enough to transport
   B. new car, which would be spacious enough to transport
   C. a new car – which would be spacious enough to transport
   D. a new car, that would be spacious enough to transport

16. Near a small river, at the bottom of the canyon we discovered a cave.
   A. river, at the bottom of the canyon we discovered a cave.
   B. river at the bottom of the canyon we discovered a cave.
   C. river at the bottom of the canyon, we discovered a cave.
   D. river, at the bottom of the canyon, we discovered, a cave.

17. Who did the interview panel select for the job?
   A. Who did the interview panel select
   B. Whom did the interview panel select
   C. Who the interview panel selected
   D. Whom the interview panel selected

18. They played the song "Always and Forever" at their wedding reception.
   A. the song "Always and Forever"
   B. the song, "Always and Forever,"
   C. the song "Always and Forever,"
   D. the song "Always and Forever",

19. He lost his scholarship, as a consequence of his poor grades.
   A. scholarship, as a consequence of his poor grades.
   B. scholarship as a consequence of his poor grades.
   C. scholarship, as a consequence his poor grades.
   D. scholarship, as a consequence of, his poor grades.

20. <u>If I was a millionaire, I would give</u> money to charity.
  A. If I was a millionaire, I would give
  B. If I was a millionaire, I will give
  C. If I were a millionaire, I would give
  D. If I were a millionaire, I will give

Rewrite the following ten sentences mentally in your own head. Follow the directions given for the formation of the new sentence. Remember that your new sentence should be grammatically correct and convey the same meaning as the original sentence.

21. *She worked all night, but she still did not finish the project.* Rewrite, beginning with: <u>Even though</u>

  The next words will be:
  A. she working all night
  B. she worked all night
  C. working all night
  D. worked all night

22. *While snow showers are common in the north during the winter, precipitation is unlikely tomorrow.* Rewrite, beginning with: <u>Despite</u>

  The next words will be:
  A. snow showers are common
  B. of snow showers being common
  C. snow showers being common
  D. snow showers as common

23. *Warm all year round, Florida has many out-of-state visitors during December and January.* Rewrite, beginning with: <u>Because</u>

  The next words will be:
  A. warm all year round,
  B. of warm all year round,
  C. of all-year-round warm,
  D. it is warm all year round,

24. *Tom is highly intelligent, and so is his younger brother.* Rewrite, beginning with: <u>Just as</u>

  Your new sentence will include:
  A. so too is his younger brother
  B. as well as his younger brother
  C. in the same way, his younger brother
  D. his younger brother, similarly

21

25. *Mary arrived at the party. Then I decided to go home.* Rewrite, beginning with: <u>After</u>

The next words will be:
A. Mary arriving at the party
B. Mary had arrived at the party
C. arriving at the party
D. arrived at the party

26. *You will succeed at college if you work hard and concentrate on your studies.* Rewrite, beginning with: <u>Provided</u>

The next words will be:
A. hard work
B. work hard
C. you work hard
D. that your work hard

27. *She is a good teacher because she is kind and patient.* Rewrite, beginning with: <u>Kind and patient</u>

Your new sentence will include:
A. of a good teacher
B. is a good teacher
C. make a good teacher
D. which a good teacher

28. *Apart from being rude, she is also stingy.* Rewrite, beginning with: <u>Besides</u>

The next words will be:
A. being rude
B. of being rude
C. of rudeness
D. she is rude

29. *The teacher became upset because the student was insolent when asked about completing the homework assignment.* Rewrite, beginning with: <u>Because of</u>

The next words will be:
A. being upset
B. the teacher was upset
C. he student was insolent
D. the student's insolence

30.   *More and more teenagers are developing type II diabetes due to poor dietary choices and a lack of physical activity.* Rewrite, beginning with: <u>Increasing</u>

The next words will be:
A.   teenagers
B.   teenage diabetes
C.   numbers of teenagers
D.   amount of teenagers

TSI WRITING PRACTICE TEST 1 – ANSWERS AND EXPLANATIONS

1. The correct answer is B. The sentences need to be grammatically correct and the clauses should be in their original order in order to give the correct emphasis to the ideas.

2. The correct answer is A. The word "however" needs to be offset with commas when used in the middle of a sentence like this one. B and D are possible answers, but not the best answers. B is not the best answer because full forms like "did not" are more common in formal writing than contractions. D is not the best answer because of the repetition of the pronoun "they." Answer C is incorrect.

3. The correct answer is C. Sentence 3 talks about the lack of independence the Pilgrims felt, which was the reason they immigrated to America. "Therefore" is the only answer choice that implies a cause and effect relationship between the two sentences, so it is the correct answer.

4. The correct answer is D. Sentence 5 talks about the Pilgrims' lack of social standing, so the lack of social status mentioned in the new sentence is mostly closely related with this idea from sentence 5.

5. The correct answer is B. Replacing the pronoun is the best choice for stylistic reasons in this instance. The sentence already contains the pronouns "their" and "them." Accordingly, the replacement of the pronoun "they" makes the sentence sound less repetitious.

6. The correct answer is C. The ideas contained in these two sentences are closely related. Sentence 6 describes a problem, while sentence 7 explains the solution. Accordingly, the two sentences should be subordinated as in sentence C. Answer A does not contain a subordinator. Answer B places the ideas in the reverse order, giving the wrong emphasis. Answer D is incorrect because "nevertheless" should be preceded by a semicolon in this instance.

7. The correct answer is D. Sentence D fits in with the chronological flow of events mentioned in the paragraph. The other answers do not.

8. The correct answer is A. Sentence 9 speaks about the Pilgrims reaching America, and sentence 10 talks about their new life. Accordingly, the new sentence, which describes the establishment of Plymouth upon their settlement in America, fits best between sentences 9 and 10 because this placement gives the paragraph the best chronological flow.

9. The correct answer is D. This is another question on subordination. Answers A and B are not the best. You should leave the ideas in their original order since the harsh winter in sentence 11 relates to the deaths mentioned in sentence 12. Answer C is not

a logical construction since no cause-and-effect relationship exists between the two sentences.

10. The correct answer is B. The final sentence is mentioning an unfortunate but not unexpected outcome, so answer B is the best choice.

11. The correct answer is D. The clause *Although she was only sixteen years old* modifies the pronoun "she." Therefore, "she" needs to come after this clause.

12. The correct answer is A. This question is an example of the inverted sentence structure. When a sentence begins with a negative phrase [no sooner, not only, never, etc.], the past perfect tense [had + past participle] must be used. In addition, the auxiliary verb "have" must be placed in front of the grammatical subject of the sentence [I].

13. The correct answer is B. This question is about "parallelism." In order to follow the grammatical rules of parallelism, you must be sure that all of the items you give in a series are of the same part of speech. So, all of the items must be nouns or verbs, for example. In other words, you should not use both nouns and verbs in a list. Answer B has all nouns, but the other answer choices have some nouns and some verbs.

14. The correct answer is D. This question is about the use of punctuation. "However, the noise next door made it impossible" is a complete sentence. It has a grammatical subject [the noise] and a verb [made]. "However" must be preceded by a period, and the new sentence must begin with a capital letter. In addition, "however" is a sentence linker. So, "however" must be followed with a comma.

15. The correct answer is A. The words "which would be spacious enough to transport her equipment" form a restrictive modifier. A restrictive modifier is a clause or phrase that provides essential information about a noun in the sentence. In other words, we would not know exactly what kind of new car she wanted without the clause "which would be spacious enough to transport her equipment." Restrictive modifiers should not be preceded by a comma.

16. The correct answer is C. The prepositional phrase "Near a small river at the bottom of the canyon" describes the location of the people when they made their discovery. So, the prepositional phrase must be followed by "we." Since the prepositional phrase is at the beginning of the sentence, the complete phrase needs to be followed by a comma.

17. The correct answer is B. This question tests your knowledge of "who" and "whom." Remember to use "who" when the person you are talking about is doing the action, but to use "whom" when the person is receiving an action. In this sentence, the candidate is receiving the action of being selected. So, the question should begin with "whom." The auxiliary verb "did" needs to come directly after "whom" to have the correct word order for this type of question.

18. The correct answer is A. The phrase "Always and Forever" is an example of a restrictive modifier. As mentioned in question number 5, restrictive modifiers are clauses or phrases that provide essential information in order to identify the subject. In other words, without the phrase "Always and Forever" in this sentence, we would not know exactly which song they played at their wedding. So, the phrase conveys essential information. Note that restrictive modifiers should not be preceded by a comma.

19. The correct answer is B. In this sentence, the word "as" functions as a subordinating conjunction. Commas should not be placed before subordinating conjunctions like this one. Other examples of subordinating conjunctions are "because" and "since."

20. The correct answer is C. If you are talking about yourself in an imaginary situation, you need to use *were* instead of *was*. This is known as the subjunctive mood. In the other half of the sentence, you need to use the verb "would" when you are describing an imaginary situation.

21. The correct answer is B. The new sentence would be constructed as follows: Even though she worked all night, she still did not finish the project. Sentences that begin with "even though" are used to introduce an unexpected result to a situation. Remember that "even though" is used to join subordinate clauses to sentences. Subordinate clauses contain a grammatical subject (she) and a verb (worked).

22. The correct answer is C. The new sentence would be constructed as follows: Despite snow showers being common in the north during the winter, precipitation is unlikely tomorrow. "Despite" takes a noun phrase, not a clause. In other words, the part of the sentence that contains "despite" should not include a verb. "Despite" should also not be followed directly by "of." In this example, the word "being" functions as an adjectival phrase, not a verb.

23. The correct answer is D. The new sentence would be constructed as follows: Because it is warm all year round, Florida has many out-of-state visitors during December and January. "Because" is a subordinator. In other words, the part of the sentence that includes "because" also needs to include a verb. Answer D contains a verb [is], but the other answers do not have verbs.

24. The correct answer is A. The new sentence is: Just as Tom is highly intelligent, so too is his younger brother. Comparative sentences that begin with "just as" need to include "so too" in the other part of the sentence.

25. The correct answer is B. The new sentence is formed as follows: After Mary had arrived at the party, I decided to go home. Clauses that begin with "After" normally need to contain the past perfect tense. The past perfect tense is formed with "had" plus the past participle, which is "arrived" in this sentence.

26. The correct answer is C. "Provided" is used in sentences in the same way as "if." So, we can replace "if" with "provided." In addition, the end of the original sentence is moved to the beginning of the new sentence. Be sure you put a comma after the "if" clause once you have changed the order of the clauses in the sentence. The new sentence is: Provided you work hard and concentrate on your studies, you will succeed at college.

27. The correct answer is B. The phrase "kind and patient" modifies the word "teacher." Therefore, your new sentence will be: Kind and patient, she is a good teacher.

28. The correct answer is A. The new sentence is constructed as follows: Besides being rude, she is also stingy. In sentences like this, you can replace the phrase "apart from" with the word "besides."

29. The correct answer is D. The new sentence is: Because of the student's insolence when asked about completing the homework assignment, the teacher became upset. Remember that "because" is a subordinator. So, "because" needs to be followed by a verb. On the other hand, "because of" is a phrase linker, so the part of the sentence that contains "because of" needs to be followed by a noun phrase. "The student's insolence" is a noun phrase.

30. The correct answer is C. The new sentence is: Increasing numbers of teenagers are developing type II diabetes due to poor dietary choices and a lack of physical activity. The word "increasing" needs to be followed by "numbers" or "amounts."

TSI READING PRACTICE TEST 2

Read the passage and then select the correct answer to the question. You need to answer based on ideas that are stated, suggested, or implied in the passage.

1. Our ability to measure brain activity is owing to the research of two European scientists. It was in 1929 that electrical activity in the human brain was first discovered. Hans Berger, the German psychiatrist who made the discovery, was despondent to find out, however, that many other scientists quickly dismissed his research. The work of Berger was confirmed three years later when Edgar Adrian, a Briton, clearly demonstrated that the brain, like the heart, is profuse in its electrical activity. Because of Adrian's work, we know that the electrical impulses in the brain, called brain waves, are a mixture of four different frequencies.

   The purpose of the passage is to describe
   A.   two opposing theories.
   B.   important research about brain activity.
   C.   a personal opinion about the work of two scientists.
   D.   the different types of brain wave frequencies.

2. In the Black Hills, four visages protrude from the side of a mountain. The faces are those of four pivotal United States' presidents: George Washington, Thomas Jefferson, Theodore Roosevelt, and Abraham Lincoln. Washington was chosen on the basis of being the first president. Jefferson was instrumental in the writing of the American Declaration of Independence. Lincoln was selected on the basis of the mettle he demonstrated during the American Civil war, and Roosevelt for his development of Square Deal policy, as well as being a proponent of the construction of the Panama Canal.

   From this passage, it seems reasonable to assume that these four presidents were chosen because
   A.   of their outstanding courage.
   B.   their faces would be esthetically sympathetic to the natural surroundings.
   C.   they helped to improve the national economy.
   D.   their work was considered crucial to the progress of the nation.

3. The student readiness educational model is based on the view that students are individuals, each operating at different levels of ability. For some students, this might mean that they are operating above the average ability level of their contemporaries, while others may be functioning at a level that is below average. There are also students who are learning at the optimum learning level because they are being challenged and learning new things, but yet they do not feel overwhelmed or inundated by the new information. According to the student readiness approach, the onus falls on teachers to create classroom learning activities that will challenge the maximum number of students.

This passage is primarily about
A.   the rationale of one particular educational method.
B.   the individuality of various students.
C.   the burdens placed on teachers.
D.   the shortcomings of teachers and students.

4. Socio-economic status, rather than intellectual ability, may be the key to a child's success later in life. Consider two hypothetical elementary school students named John and Paul. Both of these children work hard, pay attention in the classroom, and are respectful to their teachers. Yet, Paul's father is a prosperous business tycoon, while John's has a menial job working in a factory. Despite the similarities in their academic aptitudes, the disparate economic situations of their parents mean that Paul is nearly 30 times more likely than John to land a high-flying job by the time he reaches his fortieth year. In fact, John has only a 12% chance of finding and maintaining a job that would earn him even a median-level income.

We can conclude from information in this passage that
A.   academic ability is directly related to one's financial status later in life.
B.   children from high-income families are academically successful.
C.   children from affluent families are more likely to remain affluent as they grow older.
D.   most children from low-income families will get jobs in factories.

5. The pyramids at Giza in Egypt are still among the world's largest structures, even today. Equivalent in height to a 48-story building, the pyramids were constructed well before the wheel was invented. It is notable that the Egyptians had only the most primitive, handmade tools to complete the massive project. Copper saws were used to cut softer stones, as well as the large wooden posts that levered the stone blocks into their final places. Wooden mallets were used to drive flint wedges into rocks in order to split them. An instrument called an adze, which was similar to what we know today as a wood plane, was employed to give wooden objects the correct finish. The Egyptians also utilized drills that were fashioned from wood and twine. In order to ensure that the stones were level, wooden rods were joined by strips of twine to check that the surfaces of the stone blocks were flat. Finally, the stone blocks were put onto wooden rockers so that they could more easily be placed into their correct positions on the pyramid.

What is the writer's main purpose?
A.   to give a step-by-step explanation of the construction of the Giza pyramids
B.   to compare the construction of the Giza pyramids to that of modern day structures
C.   to give an overview of some of the main implements that were used to construct the Giza pyramids
D.   to highlight the importance of the achievement of the construction of the Giza pyramids

6. Earthquakes occur when there is motion in the tectonic plates on the surface of the earth. The crust of the earth contains twelve such tectonic plates, which are from four to ten kilometers in length when located below the sea, although those on land can be from thirty to seventy kilometers long. Fault lines, the places where these plates meet, build up a great deal of pressure because the plates are constantly pressing on each other. Thus, the two plates will eventually shift or separate because the pressure on them is constantly increasing, and this build-up of energy needs to be released. When the plates shift or separate, we have the occurrence of an earthquake, also known as a seismic event.

The main purpose of the passage is
A.   to investigate a geological theory.
B.   to describe the events that result in a natural phenomenon.
C.   to propose a solution to a problem.
D.   to provide background to a personal observation.

7. The Hong Kong and Shanghai Bank Corporation (HSBC) skyscraper in Hong Kong is one of the world's most famous high-rise buildings. The building was designed so that it had many pre-built parts that were not constructed on site. This prefabrication made the project a truly international effort: the windows were manufactured in Austria, the exterior walls were fabricated in the United States, the toilets and air-conditioning were made in Japan, and many of the other components came from Germany.

    The main idea of this passage is that
    A.   prefabricated buildings are more international than those built in situ.
    B.   countries should work together more often in construction projects.
    C.   the HSBC building was an international project.
    D.   the HSBC building is well-known because many countries were involved in its construction.

8. In December 406 A.D in what is now called Germany, 15,000 warriors crossed the frozen Rhine River and traveled into the Roman Empire of Gaul. A new historical epoch would soon be established in this former Roman Empire. Even though this period has diminished in historical significance in comparison to more recent events, the demise of the Roman Empire was certainly unprecedented in the fifth century. The six subsequent centuries that followed the collapse of the Roman Empire formed what we now call the Middle Ages.

    According to the passage, the Roman Empire of Gaul
    A.   was established during the middle ages.
    B.   is now referred to as Germany.
    C.   gradually collapsed throughout the Middle Ages.
    D.   fell into ruin from 406 to 499 AD.

9. The study of philosophy usually deals with two key problem areas: human choice and human thought. A consideration of both of these problem areas includes scientific and artistic viewpoints on the nature of human life. The first problem area, human choice, asks whether human beings can really make decisions that can change their futures. It also investigates to what extent the individual's future is fixed and pre-determined by cosmic forces outside the control of human beings. In the second problem area, human thought, epistemology is considered. Epistemology means the study of knowledge; it should not be confused with ontology, the study of being or existence.

    The primary purpose of the passage is
    A.   to compare two areas of an academic discipline.
    B.   to explain key aspects of a particular area of study.
    C.   to contrast scientific and artistic views on a particular topic.
    D.   to investigate two troublesome aspects of human behavior.

10. In 1859, some of Abraham Lincoln's associates began to put forward the idea that he should run for president of the United States, a notion that he discounted in his usual self-deprecating manner. Yet, as time passed, Lincoln began to write influential Republican Party leaders for their support. By 1860, Lincoln had garnered more public support, after having delivered public lectures and political speeches in various states. Despite being the underdog, Lincoln won 354 of the 466 total nominations at the Republican National Convention, and later, in November, 1860, the populace elected Lincoln as President of the United States.

This passage is mainly about
A.   the personal characteristics of Abraham Lincoln.
B.   the results of the 1860 US election.
C.   how Lincoln ran for and won the US presidency.
D.   how to be successful as a politician.

Read Passages 1 and 2 below. Then answer the questions. You need to answer based on ideas that are stated, suggested, or implied in the passage.

Passage 1:

Almost everyone has heard the hit single "Don't Worry, Be Happy" by Bobby McFerrin. The song has a very repetitive way of conveying its message. McFerrin's refrain was that everyone can feel happy if they simply choose not to worry.

Living a happy and worry-free life is a **wonderful** ideal, but it must be said that life is full of stresses and strains that are often not of our own choosing. One of the truest things ever said is that the only thing in life that will always remain the same is change.

In addition to causing us to worry, stress is also linked to the top causes of death, such as heart disease, cancer, and stroke. So, achieving happiness in today's society is often a complex, multi-dimensional process.

Passage 2:

Abraham Lincoln observed that happiness is a choice for most people. This echoes the claims of the Dalai Lama, who stated that people can decide whether they will be happy or not through self-discipline. So, isn't the choice simple really? Shouldn't we choose to be happy?

Being happy is actually an attitude. We have so much to be thankful for. Thank the taxi driver for bringing you home safely, thank the cook for a wonderful dinner, and thank the guy who cleans your windows. When we give thanks to others whenever possible, we choose the path of gratitude that leads to the road to happiness.

11. The writer of Passage 1 would probably criticize the writer of Passage 2 for
    A. taking an oversimplified view of happiness.
    B. claiming that people are not thankful enough.
    C. describing certain people's lack of self-discipline.
    D. failing to mention the impact of worry on happiness.

12. How would the writer of Passage 2 most likely respond to the following statement from Passage 1?: "It must be said that life is full of stresses and strains that are often not of our own choosing."
    A. People who experience stress are ungrateful for the positive aspects of their lives.
    B. Abraham Lincoln and the Dalai Lama also experienced stress.
    C. It may be true that we cannot choose certain events in life, but we can still choose to be happy.
    D. Stressed-out people lack self-discipline generally.

33

Read Passages 1 and 2 below. Then answer the questions. You need to answer based on ideas that are stated, suggested, or implied in the passage.

Passage 1:

Diners in restaurants sometimes ask why their servers aren't able to cope with some of their requests. Is it fair to suggest that members of the service industry typically deliver below-par service to customers? Consider a simple example of a fast food restaurant. Chances are that you've been at the receiving end of some bad service at some point in time. Is it then fair to assume that staff that wear work uniforms are simply to be tagged with a warning sign that they will not deliver to their clientele?

To fully understand the reasons for occasional bad service, the factors influencing the situation need to be considered. Perhaps the person providing the service was new to his or her job. Maybe he or she was a trainee and was not able to perform without the assistance of a supervisor. In addition, service people can experience a great deal of stress when trying to do several things at once for different patrons.

Passage 2:

Whether in the fast food service or in a legal firm, there are countless factors that can influence the outcome of the service provided. However, a person who wears a suit to work is less likely to make a mistake than someone in the service industry.

The hurried pace and pressure to perform in the service industry cause mistakes to occur. Those who do office work have the luxury of working in less stressful environments. They have more time to check their work for mistakes before delivering it to their clients.

13.   The writer of Passage 1 would probably take the most offense with which one of the following claims from Passage 2?
A.   Whether in the fast food service or in a legal firm, there are countless factors that can influence the outcome of the service provided.
B.   A person who wears a suit to work is less likely to make a mistake than someone in the service industry.
C.   The hurried pace and pressure to perform in the service industry cause mistakes to occur.
D.   Those who do office work have the luxury of working in less stressful environments.

14. How would the writer of Passage 2 most likely respond to the following rhetorical question from Passage 1: "Is it then fair to assume that staff that wear work uniforms are simply to be tagged with a warning sign that they will not deliver to their clientele?"

A. This is a fair assumption because service people generally make a great deal of mistakes in their work.

B. This is not a fair assumption because service people can't help making mistakes due to the amount of pressure they are under at work.

C. The assumption is not entirely unfounded because service people sometimes make mistakes owing to the fact that they don't have sufficient time to check their work.

D. This is an unfair assumption since work uniforms do not affect job performance.

15. The writers of both passages would agree that

A. office workers are less likely to make mistakes than service people.

B. lawyers work more conscientiously than wait staff.

C. the clothes a person wears can affect work performance.

D. the service industry can be extremely stressful at times.

Read the passage and then select the correct answers to the questions. You need to answer based on ideas that are stated, suggested, or implied in the passage.

Literary Text 1

The excellent Mr. Morris was an Englishman, and he lived in the days of Queen Victoria the Good. He was a prosperous and very sensible man; he read the Times and went to church, and as he grew towards middle age an expression of quiet contented contempt for all who were not as himself settled. Everything that it was right and proper for a man in his position to possess, he possessed.

And among other right and proper possessions, this Mr. Morris had a wife and children. They were the right sort of wife, and the right sort and number of children, of course; nothing imaginative or highty-flighty about any of them, so far as Mr. Morris could see; they wore perfectly correct clothing, neither smart nor hygienic nor faddy in any way; and they lived in a nice sensible house.

And when it was a fit and proper thing for him to do so, Mr. Morris died. His tomb was of marble, and, without any art nonsense or laudatory inscription, quietly imposing— such being the fashion of his time.

He underwent various changes according to the accepted custom in these cases, and long before this story begins his bones even had become dust, and were scattered to the four quarters of heaven. And his sons and his grandsons and his great-grandsons and his great-great-grandsons, they too were dust and ashes, and were scattered likewise. It was a thing he could not have imagined, that a day would come when even his great-great-grandsons would be scattered to the four winds of heaven. If anyone had suggested it to him he would have resented it.

He was one of those worthy people who take no interest in the future of mankind at all. He had grave doubts, indeed, if there was any future for mankind after he was dead. It seemed quite impossible and quite uninteresting to imagine anything happening after he was dead. Yet the thing was so, and when even his great-great-grandson was dead and decayed and forgotten, when the sham half-timbered house had gone the way of all shams, and all that Mr. Morris had found real and important was sere and dead, the world was still going on, and people were still going about it, just as heedless and impatient of the Future, or, indeed, of anything but their own selves and property, as Mr. Morris had been.

16.   What does the narrator imply when he states "And among other right and proper possessions, this Mr. Morris had a wife and children"?
       A.   Mr. Morris felt affection toward his wife and children, although he sometimes treated them coldly.
       B.   Mr. Morris got married and had a family because social convention dictated that he do so.
       C.   Mr. Morris quietly resented his wife and family because they made him acquire possessions that he did not want.
       D.   Mr. Morris's family awaited his passing because it meant they would come into a good inheritance.

17.   What is the best meaning of "highty-flighty" as it is used in paragraph 2?
       A.   empty-headed
       B.   erudite
       C.   sensitive
       D.   unfriendly

18.   What is the best paraphrase of this phrase: "when the sham half-timbered house had gone the way of all shams?"
       A.   when Mr. Morris was long dead and his possessions were gone and forgotten
       B.   when Mr. Morris's great-grandsons had forgotten about the house and their great-grandfather
       C.   when the precious home had decayed and was scattered like ash and dust
       D.   when the pretentious dwelling was gone and forgotten, like all worldly possessions

19.   The description of Mr. Morris's home and his tomb are similar because
       A.   they demonstrated no real interest in the future of mankind.
       B.   they displayed the underlying resentment that Mr. Morris felt about his life.
       C.   they would have been considered right and proper for the society of their time.
       D.   they both reveal the heed and care that society takes about the future.

20.   From the tone of this passage, the reader could assume that the story is going to be about
       A.   how life in the future is different than life in the past.
       B.   the narrator's regrets with his grandchildren.
       C.   the protagonist's home and other possessions.
       D.   spiritual aspects of the afterlife.

Read the passage and then select the correct answers to the questions. You need to answer based on ideas that are stated, suggested, or implied in the passage.

Literary Text 2

Oliver, having taken down the shutters, was graciously assisted by Noah, who having consoled him with the assurance that "he'd catch it," condescended to help him. Mr. Snowberry came down soon after.

Shortly afterwards, Mrs. Snowberry appeared. Oliver having "caught it," in fulfillment of Noah's prediction, followed the young gentleman down the stairs to breakfast.

"Come near the fire, Noah," said Charlotte. "I have saved a nice little bit of bacon for you from master's breakfast."

"Do you hear?" said Noah.

"Lord, Noah!" said Charlotte.

"Let him alone!" said Noah. "Why everybody lets him alone enough, for the matter of that."

"Oh, you queer soul!" said Charlotte, bursting into a hearty laugh. She was then joined by Noah, after which they both looked scornfully at poor Oliver Twist.

Noah was a charity boy, but not a workhouse orphan. He could trace his genealogy back to his parents, who lived hard by; his mother being a washerwoman, and his father a drunken soldier, discharged with a wooden leg, and a diurnal pension of twopence-halfpenny and an unstable fraction. The shop boys in the neighborhood had long been in the habit of branding Noah, in the public streets, with the ignominious epithets of "leathers," "charity," and the like; and Noah had borne them without reply. But now that fortune had cast his way a nameless orphan, at whom even the meanest could point the finger of scorn, he retorted on him with interest.

21.   What is the meaning of "he'd catch it" in the first paragraph of the passage?
    A.   he'd find it
    B.   he'd be saved
    C.   he would be laughed at
    D.   he would be punished

22. From paragraph 3, the reader can surmise that Charlotte is
    A. the Snowberry's daughter.
    B. Noah's sister.
    C. Oliver's sister.
    D. an employee of the Snowberry family.

23. According to the passage, Oliver could be described as
    A. gracious.
    B. scornful.
    C. ignominious.
    D. ridiculed.

24. The passage mainly illustrates
    A. Charlotte's contempt of orphans.
    B. the wealth of the Snowberry family.
    C. the adventures and exploits of Oliver.
    D. the relationship between Noah and Oliver.

25. Who is the "nameless orphan" mentioned in the passage?
    A. charity boys
    B. workhouse orphans
    C. Noah
    D. Oliver

TSI READING PRACTICE TEST 2 – ANSWERS AND EXPLANATIONS

1. The correct answer is B. For this type of question, you need to look carefully at the topic sentence: Our ability to measure brain activity is owing to the research of two European scientists. This sentence states that the passage is going to talk about brain research. We know that the research is important because the passage states: "Because of Adrian's work, we know that . . ."

2. The correct answer is D. The word "pivotal" in the passage means crucial to the progress of something.

3. The correct answer is A. Answer A is the most general answer. We know that the paragraph is going to talk about the rationale (or reasons for something) because it begins with the phrase "is based on the view." The other answers provide specific information from the passage.

4. The correct answer is C. The passage states: "Paul is nearly 30 times more likely than John to land a high-flying job." High-flying means well-paid, so Paul will remain affluent. The other answer choices are incorrect interpretations of specific points from the passage.

5. The correct answer is C. The writer's main purpose is to give an overview of some of the main implements that were used to construct the Giza pyramids. The main purpose of the passage is implied in the third sentence of the paragraph: "It is notable that the Egyptians had only the most primitive, handmade tools to complete the massive project." This is not a step-by-step explanation since the methods are not given in the correct order.

6. The correct answer is B. The passage gives factual information about the events that cause an earthquake, which is a natural phenomenon. There is no investigation, proposal, or personal observation.

7. The correct answer is C. The passage states: "This prefabrication made the project a truly international effort." Ideas from answers A and B are not mentioned in the passage. The passage does not give the precise reason why the building is famous. It just states that the building is famous.

8. The correct answer is D. The passage states: "the demise of the Roman Empire was certainly unprecedented in the fifth century." We know that "demise" means ruin. We also know that the invasion took place in 406 AD, and that the fifth century ended in 499 AD.

9. The correct answer is B. The topic sentence states: "The study of philosophy usually deals with two key problem areas." The passage does not make any comparisons or contrasts, nor does it describe human behavior as "troublesome." It merely describes the key areas as "problem areas."

10. The correct answer is C. The main idea of the passage is to give information about how Lincoln became the president. Answers A and B are too specific, and answer D is an overgeneralization.

11. The correct answer is A. The writer of passage 1 asserts: "So, being happy in today's society is often a complex, multi-dimensional process." The writer of passage 2 does not mention any of the external factors or complications that impede the achievement of happiness, so his passage would be seen as somewhat one-dimensional or oversimplified by the writer of passage 2.

12. The correct answer is C. The writer of passage 2 emphasizes that personal choice is the most significant factor in being happy, so he would disagree with the idea that unhappiness can be caused by events outside of the control of human choice.

13. The correct answer is B. The writer of passage 1 poses the following rhetorical question: "Is it then fair to assume that staff that wear work uniforms are simply to be tagged with a warning sign that they will not deliver to their clientele?" She then goes on to refute this idea in the remainder of passage 1. Accordingly, the writer of passage 1 would disagree with the assertion from passage 2 that "a person who wears a suit to work is less likely to make a mistake than someone in the service industry."

14. The correct answer is C. The writer of passage 2 claims that "the hurried pace and pressure to perform in the service industry cause mistakes to occur." So, she would agree with the claim that those in the service industry sometimes do "not deliver to their clientele."

15. The correct answer is D. The writer of passage 1 mentions that "service people can experience a great deal of stress when trying to do several things at once for different patrons." The writer of passage 2 talks about "the hurried pace and pressure to perform in the service industry."

16. The correct answer is B. The passage explains how Mr. Morris conformed to social convention throughout his life. We can see this idea, for example, at the end of paragraph 1, which states: "Everything that it was right and proper for a man in his position to possess, he possessed." This idea is repeated at the beginning of paragraph 4, in the statement that: "He underwent various changes according to the accepted custom in these cases."

17. The correct answer is A. Paragraph 2 describes how Mr. Morris had "the right sort and number of children." So, the reader can assume that Mr. Morris's children, like Mr. Morris himself, conform to social convention by trying to be responsible and logical.

18. The correct answer is D. Something that is sham is used only for show or to impress others. Accordingly, the adjective "pretentious" from answer choice D is the best synonym for "sham."

19. The correct answer is C. The narrator tells us that Mr. Morris's home was "a nice sensible house," and his tomb is described as "being the fashion of his time." The reader can therefore deduce that both the house and the tomb would have been considered right and proper for the society of their time.

20. The correct answer is A. The reader can conclude that the story is going to be about how life in the future is different than life in the past because it talks about both the past and the future in the last paragraph of the passage. In addition, the word "future" is capitalized in one instance to give emphasis to this concept.

21. The correct answer is D. "He'd catch it" means that Oliver was to be punished. This interpretation is supported by paragraph 2, which implies that Mrs. Snowberry is an authoritarian whom the boys fear.

22. The correct answer is D. in the second paragraph of the text Charlotte states "I have saved a nice little bit of bacon for you from master's breakfast." In those days, the task of preparing meals and cleaning up after them would have been done by a servant, not a family member. Charlotte also refers to Mr. Snowberry as "master," so we know that she is a servant.

23. The correct answer is D. Noah exclaims about Oliver: "Let him alone!" This exclamation indicates that Oliver is the source of ridicule. The passage also mentions that Oliver is scorned, which is synonymous with being ridiculed.

24. The correct answer is D. The passage mainly illustrates the relationship between Noah and Oliver. This idea is illustrated especially clearly in the last paragraph of the passage, in which we see Noah's view of Oliver.

25. The correct answer is D. The last sentence of the passage states: "But now that fortune had cast his way a nameless orphan, at whom even the meanest could point the finger of scorn, he retorted on him with interest." In this sentence, "his" refers to Noah, so the "nameless orphan" must refer to Oliver.

TSI WRITING PRACTICE TEST 2

Read the draft essay below and then choose the best answers to the questions that follow.

(1) The major significant characteristic of any population is its age-sex structure, this is defined as the proportion of people of each gender in each different age group. **(2)** The age-sex structure of various populations have social policy implications. **(3)** For instance, a population with a high proportion of elderly citizens needs to consider its governmentally-funded pension schemes and health care systems carefully. **(4)** A demographic with a greater percentage of young children should ensure that its educational funding and child welfare policies are implemented efficaciously. **(5)** The composition of a population changes over time. **(6)** The government may need to re-evaluate its funding priorities.

(7) Low birth rates might be attributable to a governmental policy that attempts to control the population by restricting the number of children families can have. **(8)** Demographic change can also occur due to unnaturally high death rates. **(9)** After a disease epidemic or natural disaster, uncharacteristically high numbers of death are especially evident. **(10)** Finally, migration is another factor in demographic attrition, because in any population, a certain amount of people, may decide to emigrate, or move to a different country.

1.   What is the best way to revise sentence 1? Sentence 1 is provided again here for ease of reference.

The major significant characteristic of any population is its age-sex structure, this is defined as the proportion of people of each gender in each different age group.

 A.   Replace the word "this" with the word "which"
B.   Delete the word "major"
C.   Replace the word "is" with "should be"
D.   Delete the words "defined as"

2.   Where is the best place to insert the following sentence?

It is possible that a population may have an imbalance in the age-sex structure due to low birth rates, for instance.

A.   Before Sentence 7
B.   Before Sentence 8
C.   Before Sentence 9
D.   Before Sentence 10

3.   What is the error in sentence 2? Sentence 2 is provided again here for ease of reference.

The age-sex structure of various populations have social policy implications.

A.   The word "have" should be replaced with "has"
B.   The word "structure" should be replaced with "structures"
C.   The word "policy" should be replaced with "policies"
D.   The word "implications" should be replaced with "implication"

4.   Which one of the following words or phrases would be best inserted at the beginning of sentence 4? Sentence 4 is provided again here for ease of reference.

A demographic with a greater percentage of young children should ensure that its educational funding and child welfare policies are implemented efficaciously.

A.   Just as
B.   Accordingly,
C.   In contrast to
D.   On the other hand,

5.   Which of the following sentences would be best inserted between sentences 4 and 5?

A.   Young children can be precocious or even gifted.
B.   Many regard the government as capricious in its budgeting and spending decisions.
C.   In addition, a population with an increasing proportion of adults of child-bearing age may need to evaluate funding for child-birth and parenting classes.
D.   Yet, we must bear in mind that it is not feasible to provide full funding to all sectors of the population.

6. What is the best way to revise and combine sentences 5 and 6?

A. The composition of a population changes over time because the government may need to re-evaluate its funding priorities.

B. Since the composition of a population changes over time, the government may need to re-evaluate its funding priorities.

C. The composition of a population changes over time, surely, the government may need to re-evaluate its funding priorities.

D. The composition of a population changes over time so that the government may need to re-evaluate its funding priorities.

7. What is one possible way to rewrite sentence 7? Sentence 7 is provided again here for ease of reference.

Low birth rates might be attributable to a governmental policy that attempts to control the population by restricting the number of children families can have.

A. Restricting the number of children families can have, low birth rates might be attributable to a governmental policy that attempts to control the population.

B. Low birth rates, restricting the number of children families can have, might be attributable to a governmental policy that attempts to control the population.

C. Low birth rates might be attributable to a governmental policy that attempts to control the population, restricting the number of children families can have.

D. Low birth rates might be attributable to a governmental policy restricting the number of children families can have, attempting to control the population.

8. What word or phrase is best inserted at the beginning of sentence 8? Sentence 8 is provided again here for ease of reference.

Demographic change can also occur due to unnaturally high death rates.

A. Moreover,
B. In contrast,
C. Precisely,
D. For the most part,

9. What is the best revision to the phrase "uncharacteristically high numbers of death" in sentence 9?

    A.   uncharacteristically high amount of death
    B.   uncharacteristically high amount of deaths
    C.   uncharacteristically high number of deaths
    D.   uncharacteristically high numbers of deaths

10. What is the best way to punctuate sentence 10?

    A.   Finally migration is another factor in demographic attrition because in any population a certain amount of people may decide to emigrate or move to a different country.
    B.   Finally, migration is another factor in demographic attrition because, in any population a certain amount of people may decide to emigrate or move to a different country.
    C.   Finally, migration is another factor in demographic attrition, because in any population a certain amount of people, may decide to emigrate or move to a different country.
    D.   Finally, migration is another factor in demographic attrition because in any population a certain amount of people may decide to emigrate, or move to a different country.

Select the best substitute for the underlined parts of the following ten sentences. The first answer [choice A] is identical to the original sentence. If you think the original sentence is best, then choose A as your answer.

11. The child tried to grab the cookies from the <u>shelf, however they were</u> out of reach.
    A.   shelf, however they were
    B.   shelf: however they were
    C.   shelf. However, they were
    D.   shelf however, they were

12. Covered in chocolate <u>frosting, the hostess dropped the cake</u> in front of all her guests.
    A.   frosting, the hostess dropped the cake
    B.   frosting, the hostess cake dropped
    C.   frosting, the cake was dropped by the hostess
    D.   frosting, by the hostess the cake was dropped

13. <u>To love and be loved</u> is the greatest happiness of existence.
    A.   To love and be loved
    B.   Loving and be loved
    C.   Loving and to be loved
    D.   To love and being loved

14. He wanted to buy a <u>telescope, one which he could</u> use to gaze at the stars.
    A.   telescope, one which he could
    B.   telescope, which one he could
    C.   telescope one which he could
    D.   telescope. One which he could

15. No sooner <u>I had finished gardening than</u> it began to rain.
    A.   I had finished the gardening than
    B.   I finished the gardening than
    C.   had I finished the gardening
    D.   had finished I the gardening than

16. If <u>I went out</u> alone after dark, I try to be more alert and careful.
    A.   I went out
    B.   I go out
    C.   I had gone out
    D.   I were going out

17. "I am not really interested in <u>this movie" he</u> said.
    A.   this movie" he
    B.   this movie," he
    C.   this movie" . he
    D.   this movie." He

18. <u>When a person is confused about his or her identity, this</u> is known as an identity crisis.
    A.   When a person is confused about his or her identity, this
    B.   When you are confused about your identity, this
    C.   The experience of confusion about one's own identity, this
    D.   The experience of confusion about one's own identity

19. <u>Upset, from receiving the bad news, Mary</u> broke down and cried.
    A.   Upset, from receiving the bad news, Mary
    B.   Upset, from receiving the bad news Mary
    C.   Upset from receiving the bad news, Mary
    D.   Upset from receiving the bad news Mary,

Đề hỏi   *nhấn mạnh*

20. <u>Dilapidated and disheveled the house appeared</u> forlorn and abandoned.
   A.   Dilapidated and disheveled the house appeared
   B.   Dilapidated and disheveled the house, appeared
   C.   Dilapidated and disheveled the house appeared,
   D.   Dilapidated and disheveled, the house appeared

Rewrite the following ten sentences mentally in your own head. Follow the directions given for the formation of the new sentence. Remember that your new sentence should be grammatically correct and convey the same meaning as the original sentence.

21.   She wanted that new car for so long, and when she finally got it, she was so excited. Rewrite, beginning with: <u>She was excited because she</u>

   Your new sentence will include:
   A.   wanting that new car
   B.   that new car, which ✓
   C.   that new car which
   D.   which she finally got

22.   It will be easy to pass my math test, but I cannot say the same about my physics test. Rewrite, beginning with: <u>Unlike my physics test,</u>

   The next words will be:
   A.   it will be easy
   B.   I should easily
   C.   my math test
   D.   passing math

23.   She felt ill for days and eventually came down with the flu. Rewrite, beginning with: <u>Having felt</u>

   Your new sentence will include:
   A.   daily illness
   B.   eventually down she came
   C.   the flu eventually came
   D.   she eventually came down

24.   If she could afford it, she would come to Hawaii with us. Rewrite, beginning with: <u>She is not able to come to Hawaii with us</u>

   The next words will be:
   A.   because she
   B.   without her
   C.   although there
   D.   without enough

48

25. The referee blew his whistle, and then the game began. Rewrite, beginning with: <u>The game began</u>

The next words will be:
A. the referee blowing
B. and the referee
C. after the referee
D. although the referee

26. Thomas studied extensively for his final exams, but Mary did not do likewise. Rewrite, beginning with: <u>Whereas Thomas</u>

Your new sentence will include:
A. unlike Mary
B. Mary did not
C. Mary did too
D. so did Mary

27. He will only get the promotion if he receives approval from his superiors. Rewrite, beginning with: <u>Unless he receives approval from his superiors,</u>

The next words will be:
A. the promotion will be
B. he will be
C. he will get
D. he will not get

28. In spite of giving her best effort, Barbara failed to complete the project on time. Rewrite, beginning with: <u>Although</u>

The next words will be:
A. she gave
B. her effort
C. her giving
D. she failed completing

29. Sarah's father was a foreign diplomat, so she has lived in many locations around the world. Rewrite, beginning with: <u>Sarah, whose</u>

Your new sentence will include:
A. because she has lived
B. because her father was
C. she has lived in
D. has lived in

49

30. Famous for its high academic standards, Harvard attracts the best and brightest students each year. Rewrite, beginning with: <u>Because of</u>

The next words will be:
A.   the best and the brightest
B.   its high academic standards
C.   attracting the best
D.   famous for its

TSI WRITING PRACTICE TEST 2 – ANSWERS AND EXPLANATIONS

1. The correct answer is A. While the original sentence is a bit verbose, the relative pronoun "which" is needed in order to correct the comma splice.

2. The correct answer is A. Sentence 7 goes on to talk about low birth rates, which is also mentioned in the new sentence.

3. The correct answer is B. If we are talking about various populations, we are describing more than one age-sex structure, so the word "structure" needs to be given in the plural form.

4. The correct answer is D. The idea of the elderly in sentence 3 is being contrasted with the idea of young children in sentence 4, so the new phrase needs to show a contrast. The linking phrase also needs to be followed by a comma.

5. The correct answer is C. At this point, the essay is stating examples of how the composition of a population changes over time. Sentence C is the only answer that provides such an example.

6. The correct answer is B. Answer B is the only choice that is correct grammatically and that provides the correct cause-and-effect relationship between the two ideas.

7. The correct answer is C. The present participle phrase "restricting the number of children families can have" modifies the phrase "a governmental policy that attempts to control the population", so these two phrases need to be placed next to each other. In answers A, B, and D, the modifiers have been misplaced.

8. The correct answer is A. Sentence 8 is giving an additional example of the way in which the composition of a population can change. "Moreover" is the only answer choice that shows that an additional example is being given, so it is the correct answer.

9. The correct answer is D. More than one person would have died, so "death" needs to be plural in this instance. A plural form is also needed because of the verb form "are".

10. The correct answer is D. The word "finally, needs to be followed by a comma when placed at the beginning of a sentence. The phrase "or move to a different country" needs to be preceded by a comma because it provides a definition of the word "emigrate".

11. The correct answer is C. This question is about the use of punctuation. "However, they were out of reach" is a complete sentence. It has a grammatical subject [they] and a verb [were]. "However" must be preceded by a period, and the new sentence must begin with a capital letter.

Compare the placement of "however" and the punctuation in these sentences: The child tried to grab the cookies from the shelf. They were, however, out of reach. When you use the word "however" in the middle of a sentence, "however" must be preceded by a comma and also followed by a comma.

12. The correct answer is C. "Covered in chocolate frosting" is a past participle phrase that describes the cake. In other words, the hostess is not covered in chocolate frosting. Therefore, the words "the cake" must follow the past participle phrase. Remember: past participle phrases are those that begin with verbs that end in -ed (in the case of regular verbs). You need to be sure that you have the participle phrase next to the noun that the phrase is describing.

13. The correct answer is A. This is another question about "parallelism." Be sure that all of the items you give in a list are of the same part of speech, nouns or verbs, for example. In other words, you should not use both nouns and verbs in a list. In addition, all of the verbs you use must be in the same tense. In answer A, both verbs are in the "to" form. The other answers combine -ing and -ed verbs.

14. The correct answer is A. The words "one which he could use to gaze at the stars" form a dependent relative clause. A relative clause often contains "that" or "which." A dependent clause cannot stand alone as a complete sentence. Since it is a non-restrictive (non-essential) relative clause, it must be preceded by a comma.

15. The correct answer is C. This question is another example of the inverted sentence structure. When a sentence begins with a negative phrase [no sooner, not only, never, etc.], the past perfect tense [had + past participle] must be used. In addition, the auxiliary verb "had" must be placed in front of the grammatical subject of the sentence [I].

16. The correct answer is B. This question tests your knowledge of conditional sentence structures. Conditional sentences often begin with the word *if*. Conditional sentences may express generalizations, as in this sentence. Therefore, the simple present tense (go) is used in the "If" clause, and the simple present (try) is also used in the main part of the sentence. The two parts of a conditional sentence must be separated by a comma.

17. The correct answer is B. Punctuation should be enclosed within the final quotation mark when giving dialogue. The word *said* shows that the comma needed.

18. The correct answer is D. The phrase "is known as" must be preceded with a noun phrase. "The experience of confusion about one's own identity" is a noun phrase. "Is known as" must not be preceded with a verb. No comma or pronoun (e.g., this, it) is needed.

19. The correct answer is C. "Upset from receiving the bad news" modifies or describes Mary. So, this phrase must be followed with a comma. No additional commas are needed.

20. The correct answer is D. "Dilapidated and disheveled" is a past participle phrase that describes the house. Therefore, "Dilapidated and disheveled" must be followed by a comma.

21. The correct answer is B. The new sentence is: She was excited because she finally got that new car, which she had wanted for so long. We need to put a comma after "car" because "which" forms a non-restrictive relative clause. Remember that non-restrictive relative clauses convey non-essential information and that non-restrictive relative clauses must be preceded by a comma. The phrase "which she had wanted for so long" is non-essential because we have already identified the car earlier in the sentence with the phrase "that car."

22. The correct answer is C. The new sentence is: Unlike my physics tests, my math test will be easy to pass. The phrase "Unlike my physics test" is an adjectival phrase that modifies (or makes a comparison with) "my math test." Therefore, "my math test" must come directly after the comma.

23. The correct answer is D. The new sentence is: Having felt ill for days, she eventually came down with the flu. Phrases that begin with verbs in the -ing form are known as present participle phrases. In the new sentence, the present participle phrase "Having felt ill for days" modifies "she." Therefore, "she" must come directly after the comma.

24. The correct answer is A. The new sentence would be constructed as follows: She is not able to come to Hawaii with us because she cannot afford it. Remember that "because" is used to join subordinate clauses to sentences. Subordinate clauses contain a grammatical subject (she) and a verb (cannot afford), but they cannot stand alone as complete sentences.

25. The correct answer is C. The new sentence is: The game began after the referee blew his whistle. The word "after" begins the subordinate clause in the second part of the new sentence. Since the first part of the new sentence contains the past tense (began), the second part of the new sentence should also contain the past tense (blew). The words "the referee" form the grammatical subject of the subordinate clause.

26. The correct answer is B. The new sentence is: Whereas Thomas studied extensively for his final exams, Mary did not. The sentence begins with "whereas," a word which introduces a contrast or contradiction. Negative forms of the verb must be used in the second part of the sentence if the sentence begins with "whereas." So, the negative form of the verb "did not" must be used in the second part of this sentence. Therefore, answers C and D are incorrect. Answer A is incorrect because "whereas" already conveys the idea of contrast, so "unlike" would repeat the idea of contrast.

27. The correct answer is D. The new sentence is: Unless he receives approval from his superiors, he will not get the promotion. Negative forms of the verb must be used in the second part of the sentence if the sentence begins with "unless." So, the negative form of the verb "will not get" must be used in the second part of this sentence.

28. The correct answer is A. The new sentence would be constructed as follows: Although she gave her best effort, Barbara failed to complete the project on time. The word "although" is another subordinating conjunction used to join subordinate clauses to sentences.

29. The correct answer is D. The new sentence is: Sarah, whose father was a foreign diplomat, has lived in many locations around the world. The comma after "Sarah" indicates that a relative clause (e.g., whose) must be used. "Whose" is used to describe something that belongs to a person. In this sentence, we could say that Sarah's father "belongs" to her. So, the word "father" must come after "whose." Remember that relative clauses include the following words: who, which, that, whom, whose.

30. The correct answer is B. The new sentence is: Because of its high academic standards, Harvard attracts the best and brightest students each year. The phrase linker "because of" is used to join a noun phrase to a sentence. Remember that noun phrases do not contain verbs and cannot stand alone as complete sentences. Answers A and D are adjectival phrases, and answer C contains a verb. Answer B is the only choice that contains a noun phrase.

TSI READING PRACTICE TEST 3

Read the passage and then select the correct answer to the question. You need to answer based on ideas that are stated, suggested, or implied in the passage.

1. American Major League Baseball consisted of only a handful of teams when the National League was founded in 1876. Yet, baseball has grown in popularity by leaps and bounds over the years, resulting in increased ticket sales for games and bolstering the profits of its investors. The increased demand from the public, in turn, precipitated the formation of a new division, known as the American League, in 1901. Additionally, new teams have been formed from time to time in accordance with regional demand, such as was the case with the Colorado Rockies in Denver, Colorado, and the Tampa Bay Rays in Tampa Bay, Florida.

   The main purpose of the passage is
   A.   to give examples of two popular American baseball teams.
   B.   to provide specific information about the process of forming new baseball teams.
   C.   to trace historical developments relating to the popularity of baseball.
   D.   to criticize Americans who depend on baseball for entertainment.

2. The use of computers in the stock market helps to control national and international finance. These controls were originally designed in order to create long-term monetary stability and protect shareholders from catastrophic losses. Nevertheless, the high level of automation now involved in buying and selling shares means that computer-to-computer trading could result in a downturn in the stock market. Such a slump in the market, if not properly regulated, could bring about a computer-led stock market crash. For this reason, regulations have been put in place by NASDAQ, AMEX, and FTSE.

   From this passage, one could infer that
   A.   regulations on computer-to-computer trading are considered to be a financial necessity.
   B.   there are negative public views about regulations on computer-to-computer trading.
   C.   NASDAQ, AMEX, and FTSE were initially opposed to establishing regulations on computer-to-computer trading.
   D.   the role of computers in international markets has not been modified over time.

3. Airline travel is generally considered to be an extremely safe mode of transportation. Statistics reveal that far fewer individuals are killed each year in airline accidents than in crashes involving automobiles. In spite of this safety record, airlines deploy ever-increasingly strict standards governing the investigation of aircraft crashes. Information gleaned from the investigation of aircraft crashes is utilized in order to prevent such tragedies from occurring again in the future.

The main purpose of this passage is
A.   to contrast automotive travel with airline travel.
B.   to compare statistics on deaths related to transportation accidents.
C.   to explain the reasons for the investigation of aircraft crashes.
D.   to justify government spending on aircraft accident investigations.

4. In 1749, British surveyors spotted a high peak in the distant range of the Himalayas. More than 100 years later, in 1852, another survey was completed, which confirmed that this peak was the highest mountain in the world. Later named Mount Everest, this peak was considered to be the world's highest mountain until 1986. At that time, George Wallerstein from the University of Washington posited that another Himalayan mountain, named K-2, was higher than Everest. It took an expedition of Italian scientists, who used a surfeit of technological devices, to disprove Wallerstein's claim.

According to the passage, which one of the following statements is correct?
A.   Since 1749, Mount Everest has universally been considered to be the tallest mountain in the world.
B.   Wallerstein fell into disrepute in the academic community after his claims were disproved.
C.   The Italian team confirmed that Everest was, in fact, the tallest mountain in the world.
D.   In spite of a lack of technologically-advanced equipment, Italian scientists were able to refute Wallerstein's hypothesis.

5. Clones have been used for centuries in the field of horticulture. For instance, florists have traditionally made clones of geraniums and other plants by taking cuttings and re-planting them in fresh soil. Despite the predictability of cloning in the realm of plants and flowers, cloning has arguably taken on sinister undertones, thanks to the rapid development of science and technology. Some fear the ethical ramifications that will inevitably occur if cloning is extended to the human species.

We can conclude from the information in this passage that:
A.   Cloning is a somewhat controversial subject.
B.   Cloning has fallen out of favor with horticulturalists.
C.   In spite of certain misgivings, many people support human cloning.
D.   Technological advances have impeded the use of cloning.

6. Owing to the powerful and destructive nature of tornadoes, there are, perhaps not surprisingly, a number of myths and misconceptions surrounding them. For instance, many people mistakenly believe that tornadoes never occur over rivers, lakes, and oceans; yet, waterspouts, tornadoes that form over bodies of water, often move onshore and cause extensive damage to coastal areas. In addition, tornadoes can accompany hurricanes and tropical storms as they move to land. Another common myth about tornadoes is that damage to built structures, like houses and office buildings, can be avoided if windows are opened prior to the impact of the storm.

What can be inferred about the public's knowledge of tornadoes?
A.   A large number of people know how to avoid tornado damage.
B.   Most people appreciate the risk of death associated with tornadoes.
C.   Some members of the public know how to regulate the pressure inside buildings.
D.   Many people are not fully aware of certain key information about tornadoes.

7. Born in France in 1896, Jean Piaget was one of the most influential thinkers in the area of child development in the twentieth century. Piaget posited that children go through a stage of assimilation as they grow to maturity. Assimilation refers to the process of transforming one's environment in order to bring about its conformance to innate cognitive schemes and structures. Schemes used in infant breast feeding and bottle feeding are examples of assimilation because the child utilizes his or her innate capacity for sucking to complete both tasks.

Why does the writer mention bottle feeding in the above paragraph?
A.   To identify one of the important features of assimilation.
B.   To exemplify the assimilation process.
C.   To describe the importance of assimilation.
D.   To explain difficulties children face during assimilation.

8. Inherent social and cultural biases pervaded the manner in which archeological findings were investigated during the early nineteenth century because little attention was paid to the roles that wealth, status, and nationality played in the recovery and interpretation of artifacts. However, in the 1860s Charles Darwin established the theory that human beings are the ultimate product of a long biological evolutionary process. Darwinian theory infiltrated the discipline of archeology and heavily influenced the manner in which archeological artifacts were recovered and analyzed. As a result of Darwinism, there was a surge in artifacts excavated from African and Asian localities by the late 1900s.

Based on the information in the passage, what can be inferred about the early 1900s?
A.   There were few archeological findings from Africa and Asia.
B.   Darwinian theory had little effect on archeology.
C.   All archeological findings were culturally biased in the early 1900s.
D.   Charles Darwin was responsible for the recovery of many artifacts.

9. The tradition of music in the western world originated in the genre of chanting. Chant, a monophonic form of music, was the dominant mode of music prior to the thirteenth century. The semantic origins of the word "monophonic" are of special interest. "Mono" is from a Greek word which means one thing alone or by itself. "Phonic" is also Greek in origin, and it means sound. Accordingly, monophonic music consists of only one sound or voice that combines various notes in a series.

What is the main idea of this passage?
A.   The origins of music in the western world.
B.   The history of music during two previous centuries.
C.   The semantics of a particular Greek word.
D.   The variety of symphonic forms.

10. Various health risks are posed by processed or convenience food. Packaged food often contains chemicals, such as additives to enhance the color of the food or preservatives that give the food a longer life. Food additives are detrimental to health for a number of reasons. First of all, they are not natural and may perhaps be linked to disease in the long term. In addition, they may block the body's ability to absorb energy and nutrients from food, such as essential vitamins and minerals that are required for healthy bodily function.

How does the passage support its claim about food additives?
A.   By explaining their purpose.
B.   By giving reasons for their dangers.
C.   By discussing specific medical case studies.
D.   By linking them to preservatives.

Read Passages 1 and 2 below. Then answer the questions. You need to answer based on ideas that are stated, suggested, or implied in the passage.

Passage 1:

"Celebrity" is the term used to describe someone who is famous and attracts attention from the general public and the world's media. Traditionally, a celebrity would gain the title by his or her work or achievements in a particular field of expertise. Actors, musicians, politicians, and inventors have all become celebrities in the past. However, as we fall deeper and deeper into the cesspool of the twenty-first century, a new celebrity has arrived – the nobody.

As one peruses glossy TV magazines, it is easy to notice the amount of reality shows that now dominate our screens – Wife Swap, X-Factor, American Idol, America's Got Talent, and the reality pioneer Big Brother. The concept itself of Big Brother is everything that George Orwell warned us about: "normal" people are thrust into the limelight to be mocked, glorified, vilified, and humiliated in equal measures. And we lap it up.

Passage 2:

After Big Brother first hit our screens, there were several BB series. However, the housemate that is eventually voted BB winner is not necessarily the most likely to gain fame and fortune from his or her appearance on this cultural phenomenon. The champion of Big Brother earnings, who came in at second place in her series, so far has earned an estimated net worth of three million dollars. While some vilify reality TV shows and the so-called celebrity associated with them, it must nonetheless be noted that participants can change their lives with the potential income levels to be derived from appearing on reality TV.

11. How would the writer of Passage 1 most likely respond to the following statement from Passage 2?: "participants can change their lives with the potential income levels to be derived from appearing on reality TV."
     A.   Reality TV participants can earn a great deal of money, but these so-called celebrities have no real achievements or expertise.
     B.   Reality TV participants are foolish for wanting to earn money like this.
     C.   The general public needs to stop watching reality TV shows in order to avoid money being earned in this way.
     D.   Glossy TV magazines should stop promoting reality TV shows.

12. The writer of Passage 2 would criticize the writer of Passage 1 for
    A.   failing to analyze Big Brother in more depth.
    B.   failing to mention any of the positive aspects of reality shows.
    C.   calling the new celebrity a nobody.
    D.   trying to classify people as "normal."

Read Passages 1 and 2 below. Then answer the questions. You need to answer based on ideas that are stated, suggested, or implied in the passage.

Passage 1:

Resulting from the amazing success of WAP (Wireless Application Protocol) in smart phones and hand-held devices, wireless technology can have an amazing impact on your day-to-day life. These technologies help to make the mobile information society happen by blurring the boundaries between home, the office, and the outside world.

The seamless integration and connectivity that wireless technology brings with it make it possible to work more efficiently. Business users can explore a wide range of interactive services which were difficult to envisage years ago because of the complexity involved in making such devices communicate with each other.

In addition, with wireless technologies, you can get on social media wherever you are, helping us stay connected with friends and family.

Passage 2:

Recent research shows that social media platforms may actually be making us antisocial. Survey results indicate that many people would prefer to interact on Facebook or Twitter, rather than see friends and family in person. The primary reason cited for this phenomenon was that one does not need to go to the effort to dress up and travel in order to use these social media platforms.

Another independent survey revealed that people often remain glued to their hand-held devices when they do go out with friends. It therefore seems that social media platforms may be having a detrimental effect on our social skills and interpersonal relationships.

13. The writer of Passage 1 would most likely criticize the writer of Passage 2 for
    A.   relying on research results rather than anecdotal information.
    B.   placing too much emphasis on certain social media platforms.
    C.   talking about hand-held devices in particular, rather than wireless technology in general.
    D.   overlooking the positive effect that wireless technologies have had on work and office life.

14. The writer of Passage 2 would probably respond to the last sentence in Passage 1 (you . . . family.) by
    A. asserting that one should try to balance time spent on social media platforms with time spent in person with loved ones.
    B. pointing out that social media platforms are very convenient.
    C. claiming that we are actually damaging relationships with our friends and family in many cases because of wireless technologies.
    D. arguing that people should leave their hand-held devices at home when going out with friends.

15. The writers of both passages would agree that
    A. wireless technologies have impacted upon society in positive ways.
    B. social media platforms need to be used with caution.
    C. social media platforms have brought about changes to interpersonal relationships.
    D. Facebook and Twitter are useful interactive tools for business users.

Read the passage and then select the correct answers to the questions. You need to answer based on ideas that are stated, suggested, or implied in the passage.

Literary Text 1

It was the last day of July. The long hot summer was drawing to a close; and we, the weary pilgrims of the London pavement, were beginning to think of the cloud-shadows on the corn-fields, and the autumn breezes on the sea-shore.

For my own poor part, the fading summer left me out of health and out of spirits. During the past year I had not managed my professional resources as carefully as usual; and my extravagance now limited me to the prospect of spending the autumn economically between my mother's cottage at Hampstead and my own chambers in town.

The evening, I remember, was still and cloudy. It was one of the two evenings in every week which I was accustomed to spend with my mother and my sister. So I turned my steps northward in the direction of Hampstead.

The quiet twilight was still trembling on the topmost ridges of the heath; and the view of London below me had sunk into a black gulf in the shadow of the cloudy night, when I stood before the gate of my mother's cottage. I had hardly rung the bell before the house door was opened violently; my worthy Italian friend, Professor Pesca, appeared in the servant's place; and darted out joyously to receive me, with a shrill foreign parody on an English cheer.

I had first become acquainted with my Italian friend by meeting him at certain great houses where he taught his own language and I taught drawing. All I then knew of the history of his life was, that he had once held a situation in the University of Padua; that he had left Italy for political reasons (the nature of which he uniformly declined to mention to any one); and that he had been for many years respectably established in London as a teacher of languages.

I had seen him risk his life in the sea at Brighton. We had met there accidentally, and were bathing together. It never occurred to me that the art which we were practicing might merely add one more to the list of manly exercises which the Professor believed that he could learn impromptu.

16.   What does the narrator suggest in paragraph 2?
A.   that he has run out of money
B.   that he has lost all his clients
C.   that he is suffering from depression
D.   that he does not get along well with his mother

17. Why does the narrator mention his mother and sister in paragraph 3?
    A.   to imply that Hampstead is in a poorer part of the city
    B.   to foreshadow the events that will take place in his mother's cottage
    C.   to indicate a routine
    D.   to create a contrast with Professor Pesca

18. What is the best paraphrase of the following phrase from paragraph 4?:
    "appeared in the servant's place."
    A.   rang the bell for the doorman
    B.   did the job of the doorman
    C.   stood where the servant normally stands
    D.   received the servant's guests

19. What adjective best describes the narrator's relationship with Professor Pesca?
    A.   political
    B.   respectable
    C.   accidental
    D.   collegial

20. What does the narrator state or imply in the last paragraph?
    A.   Professor Pesca saved someone who was drowning.
    B.   Professor Pesca was not prone to impulsive actions.
    C.   Professor Pesca did not know how to swim.
    D.   Professor Pesca had experience working with the Coast Guard.

Read the passage and then select the correct answers to the questions. You need to answer based on ideas that are stated, suggested, or implied in the passage.

Literary Text 2

Clare, restless, went out into the dusk when evening drew on, she who had won him having retired to her chamber. The night was as sultry as the day. There was no coolness after dark unless on the grass. Roads, garden-paths, the house-fronts, the bartonwalls were warm as earths, and reflected the noontime temperature into the noctambulist's face.

He sat on the east gate of the yard, and knew not what to think of himself. Feeling had indeed smothered judgement that day. Since the sudden embrace, three hours before, the twain had kept apart. She seemed stilled, almost alarmed, at what had occurred, while the novelty, unpremeditation, mastery of circumstance disquieted him—palpitating, contemplative being that he was. He could hardly realize their true relations to each other as yet, and what their mutual bearing should be before third parties thenceforward.

The windows smiled, the door coaxed and beckoned, the creeper blushed confederacy. A personality within it was so far-reaching in her influence as to spread into and make the bricks, mortar, and whole overhanging sky throb with a burning sensibility. Whose was this mighty personality? A milkmaid's.

It was amazing, indeed, to find how great a matter the life of this place had become to him. And though new love was to be held partly responsible for this, it was not solely so. Many have learnt that the magnitude of lives is not as to their external displacements, but as to their subjective experiences. The impressionable peasant leads a larger, fuller, more dramatic life than the king. Looking at it thus, he found that life was to be seen of the same magnitude here as elsewhere.

Despite his heterodoxy, faults, and weaknesses, Clare was a man with a conscience. Tess was no insignificant creature to toy with and dismiss; but a woman living her precious life—a life which, to herself who endured or enjoyed it, possessed as great a dimension as the life of the mightiest to himself. Upon her sensations the whole world depended to Tess; through her existence all her fellow-creatures existed, to her. The universe itself only came into being for Tess on the particular day in the particular year in which she was born.

21.   The bartonwalls mentioned in paragraph 1 are most likely
    A.   an area in the garden.
    B.   a feature of the natural landscape.
    C.   a part of the house.
    D.   a path leading to one of the roads.

22. What is the meaning of the word "noctambulist" as it is used in the passage?
   A. a person who suddenly falls in love
   B. a person who responds impulsively to subjective experiences
   C. a person who experiences an external displacement
   D. a person who goes for a walk after dark

23. What is the best paraphrase of the following statement from paragraph 2: "what their mutual bearing should be before third parties thenceforward"?
   A. how they should behave to each other around other people
   B. whether or not they should support each other as a couple from this moment onwards
   C. whether or not they should kiss each other in public
   D. how they should decide whom to tell that they are now a couple

24. Where does the story take place?
   A. in a royal court
   B. in a peasant's abode
   C. in a dairy farm
   D. in a manor house

25. What does the narrator imply when he states that "Clare was a man with a conscience"?
   A. Clare has behaved poorly towards women in the past, but he repents of this behavior.
   B. Clare knows that Tess is hypersensitive, but she has to be aware of his needs.
   C. Clare understands that his life in his current environment may not be of the same magnitude that he has experienced in the past.
   D. Clare realizes that he needs to treat Tess well because she has had her own life experiences, both positive and negative.

TSI READING PRACTICE TEST 3 – ANSWERS AND EXPLANATIONS

1. The correct answer is C. We know that the passage is going to give historical information because the topic sentence [defined as the first sentence of a paragraph] contains the phrase "was founded in 1876." Answers A and B give specific points that are mentioned in the passage, not the main idea. Answer D is incorrect because no criticisms are stated in the passage.

2. The correct answer is A. The passage states that "computer-to-computer trading could result in a downturn in the stock market." Further, this downturn could result in a "computer-led stock market crash." In order to avoid these negative results, the regulations are needed. Answers B and C are not stated in the passage. Answer D is incorrect because the passage talks about how the use of computers has *changed* over time.

3. The correct answer is C. The last sentence of the passage explains the purpose of or reasons for the aircraft crash investigations. Answers A and B are too specific. Answer D is not stated in the passage.

4. The correct answer is C. The last sentence of the passage states: "It took an expedition of Italian scientists, who used a surfeit of technological devices, to disprove Wallerstein's claim." In other words, the Italians proved that Everest was in fact higher than K-2. [Note: *Surfeit* means a large or abundant amount of something.]

5. The correct answer is A. The words "sinister undertones" and "arguably" in the passage demonstrate that cloning is a controversial subject. Answer C is not implied in the passage. There is no information in the passage to suggest that answers B and D are correct.

6. The correct answer is D. The passage uses the words "myths," "misconceptions," and "mistakenly" to show that most people do not have the correct knowledge about tornadoes.

7. The correct answer is B. When explaining the idea of assimilation, the passage uses the phrase "are examples of" to show that breast and bottle feeding are being used as examples. Note that "exemplify" means to give an example.

8. The correct answer is A. The passage concludes by stating: "there was a surge in artifacts excavated from African and Asian localities by the late 1900s." "Surge" means to increase suddenly from a small or low amount. If these findings suddenly increased at the end of the century, one could assume that they were limited at the beginning of the century. Answers B and D are incorrect according to the passage. Answer C is an overgeneralization.

9. The correct answer is A. The topic sentence contains the word "originated." Only one century is mentioned in the passage, so answer B is incorrect. Answer C is too specific. Answer D is not stated in the passage.

10. The correct answer is B. The passage states: "Food additives are detrimental to health for a number of reasons." This statement is followed by two reasons: the link to disease and the blockage of nutrients.

11. The correct answer is A. The writer of passage 1 states that "Traditionally, a celebrity would gain the title by his or her work or achievements in a particular field of expertise," so he would agree with answer A.

12. The correct answer is B. The writer of passage 2 describes how participants in reality shows can "change their lives with the potential income levels to be derived from appearing on reality TV." This is an assertion about the positive, life-changing aspects of reality television. The writer of passage 1 fails to discuss any positive aspects of reality TV.

13. The correct answer is D. The writer of passage 1 talks about office life in paragraph 1 and about business users in paragraph 2. The writer of passage 2 does not mention these aspects of wireless technology.

14. The correct answer is C. The writer of passage 2 explains how people are more inclined to stay at home to chat on social media than to go out with friends and how people are glued to their hand-held devices even when they are out with friends. These are two detrimental impacts of social media on interpersonal relationships.

15. The correct answer is C. The writer of passage 1 describes the positive changes, while the writer of passage 2 describes the negative changes.

16. The correct answer is A. The narrator states in paragraph 2 that he needs to spend the autumn "economically," so the reader can surmise that he is having financial problems. Note that the narrator mentions that he is "out of spirits," but this condition is not as serious as suffering from depression.

17. The correct answer is C. The narrator says: "It was one of the two evenings in every week which I was accustomed to spend with my mother and my sister." The word "accustomed" indicates that a routine is being described.

18. The correct answer is B. The doorman would have been the servant who welcomed visitors at the front door of the house.

19. The correct answer is D. "Collegial" means acting like colleagues, or people who work in the same profession. Paragraph 5 of the text explains that Professor Pesca and the narrator met when they were teachers, so the two characters would have been colleagues.

20. The correct answer is C. The last paragraph tells us that swimming was one of the "manly exercises which the Professor believed that he could learn impromptu." The word "impromptu" means "on the spot" or "without previous practice or experience."

21. The correct answer is C. The description moves from the roads, to the garden, and then to the house. In other words, the description moves from the outdoors to the house itself, so the bartonwalls are probably a part of the house.

22. The correct answer is D. Paragraph 1 mentions that it is after dusk and that it was nighttime. We also know from paragraph 1 that Clare was restless and that he had gone out.

23. The correct answer is A. "Mutual bearing" means how they interact with each other. "Third parties" is a formal way of saying "other people."

24. The correct answer is C. We know that the story takes place in a dairy farm because Clare confesses that he has fallen in love with a milkmaid at the end of paragraph 3.

25. The correct answer is D. In the next sentence of the paragraph, the narrator tells us that "Tess was no insignificant creature to toy with and dismiss; but a woman living her precious life—a life which, to herself who endured or enjoyed it, possessed as great a dimension as the life of the mightiest to himself." This sentence describes both the positive and negative experiences in Tess's life. It implies that Clare needs to respect Tess when it states that she "was no insignificant creature to toy with and dismiss."

TSI WRITING PRACTICE TEST 3

Read the draft essay below and then choose the best answers to the questions that follow.

(1) Organic farming and organic produce create many positive outcomes for the environment.

(2) Most mainstream American consumers have reservations about organic food.

(3) The first drawback that consumers perceive is of course the cost. **(4)** Consumers with higher income levels can afford organically-grown food, but many people simply do not believe that these are worth the added expense.

(5) There are also concerns about the safety of organic food due to using cow manure and the use of other animal waste as fertilizer. **(6)** Take the case of windfall apples, which are apples that fall off the tree, these apples can be contaminated by the cow manure. **(7)** This contamination occurs because manure contains a virulent bacterium. **(8)** This bacterium is known as e-coli.

(9) Some people are reluctant to purchase organic food because they believe that it spoils too quickly. **(10)** Therefore, it may be quite some time before the purchase of organic food became the norm in American households.

1. What is the best way to revise and combine sentences 1 and 2?

    A. Organic farming and organic produce create many positive outcomes for the environment, most mainstream American consumers have reservations about organic food.

    B. Most mainstream American consumers have reservations about organic food; yet organic farming and organic produce create many positive outcomes for the environment.

    C. While organic farming and organic produce create many positive outcomes for the environment, most mainstream American consumers have reservations about organic food.

D.   Organic farming and organic produce create many positive outcomes for the environment, even though most mainstream American consumers have reservations about organic food.

2.   What is the best way to punctuate sentence 3?

    A.   The first drawback that consumers perceive is of course the cost.
    B.   The first drawback that consumers perceive is, of course the cost.
    C.   The first drawback that consumers perceive is of course, the cost.
    D.   The first drawback that consumers perceive is, of course, the cost.

3.   Which of the following sentences would be best inserted between sentences 3 and 4?
    A.   However, there are also certain advantages to organic food.
    B.   Organic food often costs 50 to 100 percent more than food produced using traditional farming methods.
    C.   Organic farming procedures in European countries are quite different than American procedures.
    D.   Business acumen is required of the organic farmer in order to understand effective market strategies.

4.   What is the error in sentence 4? Sentence 4 is provided again here for ease of reference.

    Consumers with higher income levels can afford organically-grown food, but many people simply do not believe that these are worth the added expense.

    A.   The words "can afford" should be replaced with the words "should afford"
    B.   The words "with higher income levels" should be replaced with the words "at higher level income"
    C.   The word "these" should be replaced with the word "they"
    D.   The words "these are" should be replaced with the words "it is"

5.   Where is the best place to insert the following sentence?

    Consumption of the contaminated fruit can lead to serious food poisoning or even death if the produce is not washed correctly.

    A.   After sentence 5
    B.   After sentence 6
    C.   After sentence 7
    D.   After sentence 8

6.   What is the best revision to the phrase "due to using cow manure and the use of other animal waste" in sentence 5?

    A.   due to the using of cow manure and other animal waste
    B.   due to the use of cow manure and using other animal waste
    C.   due to the use of cow manure and other animal waste
    D.   due to using cow manure and using other animal waste

7.   What is one possible way to rewrite sentence 6? Sentence 6 is provided again here for ease of reference.

    Take the case of windfall apples, which are apples that fall off the tree, these apples can be contaminated by the cow manure.

    A.   Place a period after the word "tree" and capitalize the word "these" to begin a new sentence.
    B   Remove the comma after "apples" and replace the word "which" with the word "that"
    C.   Replace the phrase "which are apples that fall" with the word "falling"
    D.   Delete the word "the" before the phrase "cow manure"

8.   What is the best way to revise and combine sentences 7 and 8?

    A.   This contamination occurs because manure contains a virulent bacterium known as e-coli.
    B.   Known as e-coli, this contamination occurs because manure contains a virulent bacterium.
    C.   This contamination, known as e-coli, occurs because manure contains a virulent bacterium.
    D.   This contamination occurs, known as e-coli, because manure contains a virulent bacterium.

9.   Which one of the following words or phrases would be best inserted at the beginning of sentence 9? Sentence 9 is provided again here for ease of reference.

    Some people are reluctant to purchase organic food because they believe that it spoils too quickly.

    A.   Namely,
    B.   For instance,
    C.   Last but not least,
    D.   In general,

10. What is the best way to revise sentence 10? Sentence 10 is provided again here for ease of reference.

Therefore, it may be quite some time before the purchase of organic food became the norm in American households.

A. Delete the word "quite"
B. Replace the word "purchase" with the word "purchasing"
C. Insert the word ":the" before the word "American"
D. Replace the word "became" with the word "becomes"

Select the best substitute for the underlined parts of the following ten sentences. The first answer [choice A] is identical to the original sentence. If you think the original sentence is best, then choose A as your answer.

11. While at the mall, <u>a paperback book was purchased by me.</u>
A. a paperback book was purchased by me.
B. the paperback book was purchased by me.
C. a paperback book's purchase was made by me.
D. I purchased a paperback book.

12. <u>We just arrived</u> at the airport when Tom's flight landed.
A. We just arrived
B. Just had we arrived
C. We had just arrived
D. Just we were arriving

13. We were going to go away on <u>vacation. And then</u> our plans changed.
A. Vacation. And then
B. vacation, then
C. vacation and then
D. vacation, and then

14. John's favorite hobbies are <u>to read and to swim.</u>
A. to read and to swim.
B. to read and swimming.
C. reading and swimming.
D. reading and to swim.

15. <u>Exasperated, Bill finally lost his temper</u> with his unruly children.
A. Exasperated, Bill finally lost his temper
B. Bill was exasperated, finally lost his temper
C. Bill, was exasperated, finally lost his temper
D. Exasperating Bill, finally lost his temper

16. He was planning on finding a new <u>apartment that</u> would accommodate all of his oversized furniture.
    A. apartment that
    B. apartment. One that
    C. apartment, that
    D. apartment so that

17. "I can't believe you won the <u>lottery", Sarah</u> exclaimed.
    A. lottery", Sarah
    B. lottery." Sarah
    C. lottery!" Sarah
    D. lottery" Sarah

18. <u>In spite of he studied hard, he</u> failed the exam.
    A. In spite of he studied hard, he
    B. In spite of studying hard, he
    C. In spite of he studying hard, he
    D. In spite of studied hard, he

19. Jane is the <u>taller of</u> her four sisters.
    A. taller of
    B. taller than
    C. most tall of
    D. tallest of

20. <u>If stealing money from your employer,</u> you could be charged with the crime of embezzlement.
    A. If stealing money from your employer,
    B. Stealing money from your employer
    C. If you steal money from your employer,
    D. If you steal money from your employer

Rewrite the following ten sentences mentally in your own head. Follow the directions given for the formation of the new sentence. Remember that your new sentence should be grammatically correct and convey the same meaning as the original sentence.

21. After checking the extent of the man's injuries, the paramedics put him into the ambulance. Rewrite, beginning with: <u>Once they</u>

    The next words will be:
    A. were checking
    B. had checked
    C. had been checking
    D. will check

22. The professor's praise of my exam score in front of the other students embarrassed me. Rewrite, beginning with: <u>I was embarrassed when</u>

    The next words will be:
    A.   the professor praised
    B.   the professor praising
    C.   the professor, praising
    D.   the professor, he praised

23. Both Minnesota and Wisconsin get extremely cold in the winter. Rewrite, beginning with: <u>Like Minnesota,</u>

    The next words will be:
    A.   Wisconsin gets
    B.   and Wisconsin
    C.   extreme cold
    D.   it is

24. Rich in natural beauty and abundant in wildlife, the Grand Canyon is a popular tourist destination. Rewrite, beginning with: <u>The Grand Canyon</u>

    Your new sentence will include:
    A.   because being
    B.   because it being
    C.   because it is
    D.   because being it

25. My sister was ill with the flu, so she stayed home from school. Rewrite, beginning with: <u>My sister,</u>

    The next words will be:
    A.   ill and
    B.   she was ill
    C.   was ill
    D.   who was ill

26. If it rains tomorrow, we will have to cancel the picnic. Rewrite, beginning with: <u>In the event of</u>

    The next words will be:
    A.   raining
    B.   rains
    C.   rain
    D.   it rains

27.   The team lost the championship game, and the players were so disappointed. Rewrite, beginning with: <u>The team was</u>

Your new sentence will include:
A.   although it lost
B.   when it lost
C.   and it lost
D.   because the loss of

28.   Despite years of training, he was not selected for the Olympics. Rewrite, beginning with: <u>Although</u>

The next words will be:
A.   he trained for years
B.   training for years
C.   years of training
D.   years he trained

29.   As he watched television, he fell asleep and began snoring. Rewrite, beginning with: <u>Watching</u>

The next words will be:
A.   television he fell
B.   and fell
C.   television, he fell
D.   television, and falling

30.   Many international students suffer from homesickness during their studies in the United States. Rewrite, beginning with: <u>Suffering from</u>

Your new sentence will include:
A.   common international student's
B.   is common studying
C.   is commonality of international students
D.   is common among international students

TSI WRITING PRACTICE TEST 3 – ANSWERS AND EXPLANATIONS

1. The correct answer is C. This is another example of how to subordinate two sentences.

2. The correct answer is D. The phrase "of course" needs to be preceded and followed by commas when used in the middle of a sentence like this.

3. The correct answer is B. We are talking here about the cost of organic food, so the new sentence needs to address this topic.

4. The correct answer is D. "Food" is a singular noun, so the singular pronoun "it" is needed here.

5. The correct answer is B. We are speaking about the apples at this juncture, so the new sentence must be placed after sentence 6, which also talks about the apples.

6. The correct answer is C. This is another question on parallelism, which means that you have to use the same form when giving items in a list or series. Answers A and B are not the best because we can put "use" or "using" in the new sentence, but not both forms. Sentence D is not the best answer because it is repetitious.

7. The correct answer is A. "These apples can be contaminated by the cow manure" is a complete sentence, so the word "these" needs to be capitalized. The sentence preceding it needs to end in a period to avoid making a comma splice.

8. The correct answer is A. E-coli describes the bacterium, not the contamination, so the phrase "known as e-coli" needs to be placed after the word "bacterium". The other sentences misplace the modifier.

9. The correct answer is C. The text has talked about the disadvantages of organic food. We are talking here about the final disadvantage, so we need a phrase to indicate that we are drawing the discussion to a close.

10. The correct answer is D. We are making a prediction about a habitual action in the future, so we need to use the present simple tense of the verb "becomes".

11. The correct answer is D. The phrase *while at the mall* modifies the pronoun "I." So, "I" needs to come after this phrase.

12. The correct answer is C. When a compound sentence contains the word "just" to describe an action that has recently been completed, the past perfect tense [had + past participle] should be used in the part of the sentence containing the word "just."

13. The correct answer is D. This question is about the use of punctuation. "Then our plans changed" is an independent clause. It has a grammatical subject [our plans] and a verb [changed]. According to traditional rules of grammar, "and" is a coordinating conjunction, used to combine phrases or clauses within a sentence. Since "and" is a conjunction, we should avoid beginning sentences with "and." So, the word "and" should be included within a single sentence and preceded by a comma.

14. The correct answer is C. This question is about gerunds, also known as -ing words or verbal nouns. Note that the -ing form is usually used when discussing activities or hobbies.

15. The correct answer is A. Exasperated is a past participle phrase that describes Bill. So, the sentence is correct as it is written.

16. The correct answer is A. The words "that would accommodate all of his oversized furniture" form a dependent relative clause. A dependent relative clause containing "that" is not preceded by a comma.

17. The correct answer is C. Punctuation should be enclosed within the final quotation mark when giving dialogue. The word *exclaimed* shows that the exclamation point is needed.

18. The correct answer is B. The phrase "in spite of" must be followed by a noun or noun phrase. "In spite of" should not be followed by a clause. The -ing form "studying" is used as a gerund (a verbal noun) in this sentence.

19. The correct answer is D. This question tests your knowledge of the comparative and superlative forms. Use the comparative form (-er) when comparing two things. If you are comparing more than two things, you must use the superlative form (-est).

20. The correct answer is C. This question tests your knowledge of conditional sentence structures. Conditional sentences often begin with the word *if*. Conditional sentences may address hypothetical or imaginary situations. This sentence mentions a hypothetical situation. Therefore, the simple present tense (steal) is used in the "If" clause, and the modal verb (could) is used in the main part of the sentence. The two parts of conditional sentences beginning with "if" must be separated by a comma.

21. The correct answer is B. The new sentence is: Once they had checked the extent of the man's injuries, the paramedics put him into the ambulance. Clauses that begin with "once" need to contain the past perfect tense. The past perfect tense is formed with "had" plus the past participle, which is "checked" in this sentence.

22. The correct answer is A. The new sentence is: I was embarrassed when the professor praised my exam score in front of the other students. The word "when" forms a subordinate clause in the second part of the new sentence. Since the first part of the new sentence contains the past tense (was), the second part of the new sentence also contains the past tense (praised). The words "the professor" form the grammatical subject of the subordinate clause. Therefore, the pronoun "he" is not needed.

23. The correct answer is A. The new sentence is: Like Minnesota, Wisconsin gets extremely cold in the winter. The phrase "like Minnesota" is an adjectival phrase that modifies the noun "Wisconsin." Therefore, "Wisconsin" must come directly after the comma.

24. The correct answer is C. The new sentence is: The Grand Canyon is a popular tourist destination because it is rich in natural beauty and abundant in wildlife. The word "because" is used to join a subordinate clause to a sentence. Remember that clauses are distinct from phrases because clauses contain both a grammatical subject and a verb. "It" is the grammatical subject in the subordinate clause of the new sentence and "is" is the verb.

25. The correct answer is D. The new sentence is: My sister, who was ill with the flu, stayed home from school. The comma after "my sister" indicates that a relative clause must be used. Remember that relative clauses can include the following words: who, which, that, whom, whose.

26. The correct answer is C. The new sentence is: In the event of rain tomorrow, the picnic will have to be canceled. The phrase "in the event of" should be followed by a noun or noun phrase. In addition, the verb must be changed to the passive from, using the verb "be."

27. The correct answer is B. The new sentence would be constructed as follows: The team was so disappointed when it lost the championship game.

28. The correct answer is A. The new sentence would be constructed as follows: Although he trained for years, he was not selected for the Olympics. Sentences that begin with "although" introduce an unexpected result to a situation.

29. The correct answer is C. The new sentence is: Watching television, he fell asleep and began snoring. Phrases that begin with verbs in the -ing form are known as present participle phrases. In the new sentence, the present participle phrase "watching television" modifies "he." Therefore, "he" must come directly after the comma.

30. The correct answer is D. The new sentence is as follows: Suffering from homesickness is common among international students who study in the United States. In the new sentence, the -ing form (suffering) is used as a gerund. So, "suffering from homesickness" is the grammatical subject of the new sentence. The grammatical subject is followed by a verb (is) and an adjective (common). Note that "commonality" is a noun.

TSI TEXAS SUCCESS INITIATIVE – ESSAY WRITING GUIDE

Essay Structure

Most teachers agree that the best essays follow a four or five paragraph format. This format will help to insure that your essay is well-organized. This format also helps you write longer and more developed essays.

The five paragraph essay is organized as follows:

Paragraph 1 – This paragraph is the introduction to your essay. It should include a thesis statement that clearly indicates your main idea. It should also give the reader an overview of your supporting points. A thesis statement is a sentence that asserts the main idea of your essay.

The best thesis statements are those that contain a central idea that will serve to narrow the focus of the essay and control the flow ideas within it. As such, a thesis statement should not be too general or vague.

A good structure for the thesis statement is to think of it in terms of an assertion plus a reason or explanation. This structure is better than just giving your assertion or opinion on its own because your explanation indicates the direction that your writing is going to take.

You can think of the essay introduction like a funnel: wide at the top and narrow at the bottom. In other words, start off your introduction in a general but interesting way, and then narrow it down to your main idea and specific supporting points. Remember that the introduction announces your main idea and supporting points, while your main body develops them.

Paragraph 2 – The second paragraph is where you elaborate on your first supporting point. It is normally recommended that you state your strongest and most persuasive point in this paragraph.

Paragraph 3 – You should elaborate on your main idea in the third paragraph by providing a second supporting point.

Paragraph 4 – You should mention your third supporting point in the fourth paragraph. This can be the supporting point that you feel to be the weakest.

Paragraph 5 – In the fifth and final paragraph of the essay, you should make your conclusion. The conclusion should reiterate your supporting points and sum up your position.

The four paragraph essay will follow the same structure as above, with paragraphs 2 and 3 elaborating two key supporting points and paragraph 4 stating the conclusion. If you decide to put four paragraphs in your essay instead of five, each paragraph should be longer and slightly more detailed than that of a five paragraph essay.

Essay FAQs

How long should each body paragraph be?

For a four paragraph essay, each body paragraph should range from 120 to 170 words. For a five paragraph essay, each body paragraph should be from 100 to 140 words.

What is an elaborating idea?

Elaborating ideas include both explanations and examples. Providing clear examples to support your points is extremely important.

Each of your main body paragraphs should contain an example that supports your line of argument.

You should elaborate on and explain your example in order to make your essay persuasive.

How do elaborating ideas help to raise my essay score?

Elaboration lengthens your essay and gives you more opportunities to demonstrate higher-level grammar, complex sentence construction, and academic vocabulary.

How many elaborating ideas should I have in each paragraph?

This roughly equates to two or three elaborating ideas for each body paragraph.

How do I write the conclusion to the essay?

Conclusions can consist of as few as two sentences, provided that the sentences are cohesive, coherent, and well-constructed.

As in other parts of your essay, you will need to reiterate certain concepts in the conclusion, without repeating word for word what you have already written.

Using Linking Words and Subordination to Build Sentences

In order to perform well on the essay component of the exam, you will need to write long and developed sentences.

Sentence linking words can help you combine short sentences together to create more complex sentence structures.

Sentence linking words and phrases fall into three categories: sentence linkers, phrase linkers, and subordinators.

In order to understand how to use these types of sentence linking words and phrases correctly, you will need to know some basics of English grammar.

The basic grammatical principles for these concepts are explained in this section. Be sure to study the examples carefully before you attempt the exercises in the following section.

TYPE 1 – SENTENCE LINKERS:

Sentence linkers are used to link two complete sentences together. A complete sentence is one that has a grammatical subject and a verb.

Sentence linkers are usually placed at the beginning of a sentence and are followed by a comma.

They can also be preceded by a semicolon and followed by a comma when joining two sentences together. When doing so, the first letter of the first word of the second sentence must not be capitalized.

Sentence linker examples:

You need to enjoy your time at college. *However*, you should still study hard.

You need to enjoy your time at college; *however*, you should still study hard.

In the examples above, the grammatical subject of the first sentence is "you" and the verb is "need to enjoy".

In the second sentence, "you" is the grammatical subject and "should study" is the verb.

TYPE 2 – PHRASE LINKERS:

In order to understand the difference between phrase linkers and sentence linkers, you must first be able to distinguish a sentence from a phrase.

A phrase linker must be followed by a phrase, while a sentence linker must be followed by a sentence.

The basic distinction between phrases and sentences is that phrases do not have both grammatical subjects and verbs, while sentences contain grammatical subjects and verbs.

Here are some examples of phrases:

Her beauty and grace

Life's little problems

A lovely summer day in the month of June

Working hard

Being desperate for money

Note that the last two phrases above use the –ing form, known in these instances as the present participle.

Present participle phrases, which are often used to modify nouns or pronouns, are sometimes placed at the beginning of sentences as introductory phrases.

Here are some examples of sentences:

Mary worked all day long.

My sister lives in Seattle.

Wintertime is brutal in Montana.

"Mary," "my sister," and "wintertime" are the grammatical subjects of the above sentences.

Remember that verbs are words that show action or states of being, so "worked," "lives," and "is" are the verbs in the three sentences above.

Look at the examples that follow:

Phrase linker example 1 – no comma: He received a promotion *because of* his dedication to the job.

"His dedication to the job" is a noun phrase.

Phrase linker example 2 – with comma: *Because of* his dedication to the job, he received a promotion.

When the sentence begins with the phrase linker, we classify the sentence as an inverted sentence.

Notice that you will need to place a comma between the two parts of the sentence when it is inverted.

TYPE 3 – SUBORDINATORS:

Subordinators must be followed by an independent clause. Subordinators cannot be followed by a phrase.

The two clauses of a subordinated sentence must be separated by a comma.

The structure of independent clauses is similar to that of sentences because independent clauses contain a grammatical subject and a verb.

<u>Subordinator examples:</u>

Although he worked hard, he failed to make his business profitable.

He failed to make his business profitable, *although* he worked hard.

There are two clauses: "He worked hard" and "he failed to make his business profitable."

The grammatical subjects in each clause are the words "he", while the verbs are "worked" and "failed."

Now look at the sentence linking words and phrases below. Note which ones are sentence linkers, which ones are phrase linkers, and which ones are subordinators.

Then refer to the rules above to remember the grammatical principles for sentence linkers, phrase linkers, and subordinators.

<u>Sentence linkers for giving additional information</u>

further

furthermore

apart from this

what is more

in addition

additionally

in the same way

moreover

Sentence linkers for giving examples

for example

for instance

in this case

in particular

more precisely

namely

in brief

in short

Sentence linkers for stating the obvious

obviously

clearly

naturally

of course

surely

after all

Sentence linkers for giving generalizations

in general

on the whole

as a rule

for the most part

generally speaking

in most cases

<u>Sentence linkers for stating causes and effects</u>

thus

accordingly

hence

therefore

in that case

under those circumstances

as a result

for this reason

as a consequence

consequently

in effect

<u>Sentence linkers for concession or unexpected results</u>

however

nevertheless

meanwhile

<u>Sentence linkers for giving conclusions</u>

finally

to conclude

lastly

in conclusion

Sentence linkers for contrast

on the other hand

on the contrary

alternatively

rather

Sentence linkers for paraphrasing or restating

in other words

that is to say

that is

Sentence linkers for showing similarity

similarly

in the same way

likewise

Phrase linkers for giving additional information

besides

in addition to

Phrase linkers for stating causes and effects

because of

due to

owing to

Phrase linkers for concession or unexpected results

despite

in spite of

Phrase linkers for comparison

compared to

like

Phrase linkers for contrast

in contrast to

instead of

rather than

without

Subordinators

although

as

because

but

due to the fact that

even though

since

so

so that

once

unless

until

when

whereas

while

not only . . . but also

Time words that can be used both as phrase linkers and subordinators

after

before

Special cases

yet –"Yet" can be used as both a subordinator and as a sentence linker.

in order to – "In order to" must be followed by the base form of the verb.

thereby – "Thereby" must be followed by the present participle.

Using Linking Words and Subordination to Build Sentences – Exercises

Look at the pairs of sentences in the exercises below. Make new sentences, using the phrase linkers, sentence linkers, and subordinators provided. In many cases, you will need to create one single sentence from the two sentences provided. You may need to change or delete some of the words in the original sentences.

Exercise 1:

The temperature was quite high yesterday.

It really didn't feel that hot outside.

Write new sentences beginning as follows:

a) In spite of . . .

Hint: You need to change the form of the verb "was" in answer (a).

b) The temperature . . .

You need to include the word "nevertheless" in answer (b). Be careful with punctuation and capitalization in your answer.

Exercise 2:

Our star athlete didn't receive a gold medal in the Olympics.

He had trained for competition for several years in advance.

Write new sentences beginning as follows:

a) Our star athlete . . . .

Answer (a) should contain the word "although."

b) Despite . . .

Exercise 3:

There are acrimonious relationships within our extended family.

Our immediate family decided to go away on vacation during the holiday season to avoid these conflicts.

Write new sentences beginning as follows:

a) Because of . . .

b) Because . . .

c) Due to the fact that . . .

Exercise 4:

My best friend had been feeling extremely sick for several days.

She refused to see the doctor.

Write new sentences beginning as follows:

a) My best friend . . .

Answer (a) should contain the word "however."

b) My best friend . . .

Answer (b) should contain the word "but."

Be careful with capitalization and punctuation in your answers.

Exercise 5:

He generally doesn't like drinking alcohol.

He will do so on social occasions.

Write new sentences beginning as follows:

a) While . . .

b) He generally . . .

Answer (b) should contain the word "yet."

Exercise 6:

The government's policies failed to stimulate spending and expand economic growth.

The country slipped further into recession.

Write new sentences beginning as follows:

a) The government's policies . . .

Answer (a) should contain the word "thus."

b) The government's policies . . .

Answer (b) should contain the word "so."

Exercise 7:

Students may attend certain classes without fulfilling a prerequisite.

Students are advised of the benefit of taking at least one non-required introductory course.

Write new sentences beginning as follows:

a) Even though . . .

b) Students may attend . . .

Answer (b) should contain the phrase "apart from this."

Exercise 8:

There have been advances in technology and medical science.

Infant mortality rates have declined substantially in recent years.

Write new sentences beginning as follows:

a) Owing to . . .

b) Since . . .

Exercise 9:

It was the most expensive restaurant in town.

It had rude staff and provided the worst service.

Write new sentences beginning as follows:

a) It was the most . . .

Answer (a) should contain the word "besides."

b) In addition to . . .

Exercise 10:

Now try to combine these three sentences:

The judge did not punish the criminal justly.

He decided to grant a lenient sentence.

He did not send out a message to deter potential offenders in the future.

Write new sentences as follows:

a) Instead of . . . and thereby . . .

b) Rather than . . . in order to . . .

Before you attempt your answer, look for the cause and effect relationships among the three sentences.

In other words, which event came first? Which ones were second and third in the chain of events?

Also be careful with punctuation in your answers.

Using Linking Words and Subordination to Build Sentences – Answers

Exercise 1:

The temperature was quite high yesterday.

It really didn't feel that hot outside.

Answer (a):

a) In spite of the temperature being quite high yesterday, it really didn't feel that hot outside.

The words "in spite of" are a phrase linker, not a sentence linker.

That is to say, "in spite of" needs to be followed by a phrase, not a clause.

The verb "was" needs to be changed to "being" in order to form a present participle phrase.

Present participle phrases are made by using the –ing form of the verb. We will see this construction again in some of the following answers.

Answer (b):

There are two possible answers:

b) The temperature was quite high yesterday. Nevertheless, it really didn't feel that hot outside.

b) The temperature was quite high yesterday; nevertheless, it really didn't feel that hot outside.

"Nevertheless" is a sentence linker. As such, it needs to be used to begin a new sentence.

Alternatively, the semicolon can be used to join the original sentences. If the semicolon is used, the first letter of the word following it must not be capitalized.

Exercise 2:

Our star athlete didn't receive a gold medal in the Olympics.

He had trained for competition for several years in advance.

Answer (a):

a) Our star athlete didn't receive a gold medal in the Olympics, although he had trained for competition for several years in advance

"Although" is a subordinator, so the two sentences can be combined without any changes.

Answer (b):

b) Despite having trained for competition for several years in advance, our star athlete didn't receive a gold medal in the Olympics.

"Despite" is a phrase linker. As we have seen in answer (a) of exercise 1 above, phrase linkers need to be followed by phrases, not clauses.

The two parts of the sentence are inverted, and the verb "had" needs to be changed to "having" to make the present participle form.

Exercise 3:

There are acrimonious relationships within our extended family.

Our immediate family decided to go away on vacation during the holiday season to avoid these conflicts.

Answer (a):

a) Because of acrimonious relationships within our extended family, our immediate family decided to go away on vacation during the holiday season to avoid these conflicts.

"Because of" is a phrase linker. As such, the subject and verb (there are) need to be removed from the original sentence in order to form a phrase.

Answer (b):

b) Because there are acrimonious relationships within our extended family, our immediate family decided to go away on vacation during the holiday season to avoid these conflicts.

Answer (c):

c) Due to the fact that there are acrimonious relationships within our extended family, our immediate family decided to go away on vacation during the holiday season to avoid these conflicts.

"Because" and "due to the fact that" are subordinators, so no changes to the original sentences are required.

The phrase "to avoid these conflicts" can be omitted since this idea is already implied by the words "acrimonious relationships."

Exercise 4:

My best friend had been feeling extremely sick for several days.

She refused to see the doctor.

Answer (a):

There are two possible answers.

a) My best friend had been feeling extremely sick for several days. However, she refused to see the doctor.

a) My best friend had been feeling extremely sick for several days; however, she refused to see the doctor.

Like "nevertheless" in exercise 1, the word "however" is a sentence linker. Remember that sentence linkers need to be used at the beginning of a new sentence.

Alternatively, the semicolon can be used to join the original sentences. If the semicolon is used, "however" must not begin with a capital letter and needs to be followed by a comma.

Answer (b):

b) My best friend had been feeling extremely sick for several days, but she refused to see the doctor.

"But" is a subordinator, so the two sentences can be combined without any changes.

Exercise 5:

He generally doesn't like drinking alcohol.

He will do so on social occasions.

Answer (a):

a) While he generally doesn't like drinking alcohol, he will do so on social occasions.

Like "although," the word "while" is a subordinator, so no changes to the original sentences are needed.

Answer (b):

"Yet" can be used as both a subordinator and as a sentence linker, so there are three possible answers in this instance.

When used as a sentence linker, the sentence construction is similar to the sentences containing nevertheless" from exercise 1 and "however" from exercise 4.

Accordingly, these are two possible answers:

b) He doesn't like drinking alcohol. Yet, he will do so on social occasions.

b) He doesn't like drinking alcohol; yet, he will do so on social occasions.

A third possible answer is to use "yet" as a subordinator:

b) He doesn't like drinking alcohol, yet he will do so on social occasions.

The difference is that the third sentence places slightly less emphasis on the particular occasions in which he will drink than the other two sentences.

Exercise 6:

The government's policies failed to stimulate spending and expand economic growth.

The country slipped further into recession.

Answer (a):

"Thus" is a sentence linker, so there are two possible answers:

a) The government's policies failed to stimulate spending and expand economic growth. Thus, the country slipped further into recession.

a) The government's policies failed to stimulate spending and expand economic growth; thus, the country slipped further into recession.

Answer (b):

b) The government's policies failed to stimulate spending and expand economic growth, so the country slipped further into recession.

"So" is a subordinator. The two sentences may therefore be joined without any changes.

Exercise 7:

Students may attend certain classes without fulfilling a prerequisite.

Students are advised of the benefit of taking at least one non-required introductory course.

Answer (a):

There are two possible answers.

a) Even though students may attend certain classes without fulfilling a prerequisite, they are advised of the benefit of taking at least one non-required introductory course.

a) Even though students are advised of the benefit of taking at least one non-required introductory course, they may attend certain classes without fulfilling a prerequisite.

"Even though" is a subordinator, so no changes are needed. It is advisable to change the word "students" to the pronoun "they" on the second part of the new sentence in order to avoid repetition.

The order or the clauses may be changed in the new sentence since there is no cause and effect relationship between the two original sentences.

Answer (b):

There are two possible answers:

b) Students may attend certain classes without fulfilling a prerequisite. Apart from this, they are advised of the benefit of taking at least one non-required introductory course.

b) Students may attend certain classes without fulfilling a prerequisite; apart from this, they are advised of the benefit of taking at least one non-required introductory course.

"Apart from this" is a sentence linker, so it needs to be used at the beginning of a separate sentence.

Exercise 8:

There have been advances in technology and medical science.

Infant mortality rates have declined substantially in recent years.

Answer (a):

a) Owing to advances in technology and medical science, infant mortality rates have declined substantially in recent years.

"Owing to" is a phrase linker that shows cause and effect. In this case the cause is advances in technology and medical science, and the effect or result is the decline in infant mortality rates.

Since "owing to" is a phrase linker, the grammatical subject of the original sentence (there) and the verb (have been) are removed when creating the new sentence.

Answer (b):

b) Since there have been advances in technology and medical science, infant mortality rates have declined substantially in recent years.

"Since" is a subordinator, so you can combine the sentences without making any changes.

Remember to use the comma between the two parts of the sentence because the clauses have been inverted.

Exercise 9:

It was the most expensive restaurant in town.

It had rude staff and provided the worst service.

Answer (a):

a) It was the most expensive restaurant in town, besides having rude staff and providing the worst service.

"Besides" is a phrase linker, so use the present participle form of both verbs in the second original sentence. Accordingly, "had" becomes "having" and "provide" becomes "providing."

Answer (b):

There are two possible answers.

b) In addition to being the most expensive restaurant in town, it had rude staff and provided the worst service.

b) In addition to having rude staff and providing the worst service, it was the most expensive restaurant in town.

"In addition to" is a phrase linker, so the present participle forms are used in the phrase containing this word.

The order of the original sentences can be changed since there is no cause and effect relationship between these ideas.

Exercise 10:

Now try to combine these three sentences:

The judge did not punish the criminal justly.

He decided to grant a lenient sentence.

He did not send out a message to deter potential offenders in the future.

Answer (a):

a) Instead of punishing the criminal justly and thereby sending out a message to deter potential offenders in the future, the judge decided to grant a lenient sentence.

Answer (b):

b) Rather than punishing the criminal justly in order to send out a message to deter potential offenders in the future, the judge decided to grant a lenient sentence.

As you will see, answers A and B are somewhat similar in their construction.

"Instead of" and "rather than" need to be used with the present participle form (punishing).

"Thereby" must be followed by the present participle form (sending).

However, "in order to" needs to take the base form of the verb (send).

The base form is the verb before any change has been made to it, like making the –ed or –ing forms. The following are examples of base forms of verbs: eat, sleep, work, play.

Using Correct Grammar and Punctuation

Mechanical conventions are the rules of grammar and punctuation that are necessary in order to write accurately and correctly.

This section is intended as a basic overview of some of the most important mechanical conventions.

Comparatives and Superlatives – Avoid Using Double Forms:

Use the comparative form when comparing two things.

The comparative form consists of the adjective plus –er when the adjective has two syllables or less.

pretty → prettier

Avoid making a double comparative:

INCORRECT: more prettier

When the adjective has more than two syllables, the adjective should be preceded by the word "more" in order to form the comparative.

beautiful → more beautiful

Examples:

Tom is taller than his brother.

Tom is more intelligent than his brother.

If you are comparing more than two things, you must use the superlative form.

As a general rule, the superlative form consists of the adjective plus –est when the adjective has two syllables or less.

pretty → prettiest

Avoid making a double superlative:

INCORRECT: most prettiest

To form the superlative for adjectives that have more than two syllables, the adjective should be preceded by the word "most".

beautiful → most beautiful

Examples:

Tom is the tallest boy in his class.

Tom is the most intelligent boy in his class.

Correct Use of *Its* and *It's*:

"Its" is a possessive pronoun, while "it's" is a contraction of "it is."

CORRECT: It's high time you started to study.

INCORRECT: Its high time you started to study.

The sentence could also be stated as follows: It is high time that you started to study.

Since the contracted form of "it is" is used in the alternative sentence, "it's" is the correct form.

CORRECT: A snake sheds its skin at least once a year.

INCORRECT: A snake sheds it's skin at least once a year.

"Its" is a possessive pronoun referring to the snake, so the apostrophe should not be used.

Correct Use of *Their*, *There*, and *They're*:

"Their" is a plural possessive pronoun.

"There" is used to describe the location of something.

"They're" is a contraction of "they are."

CORRECT: Their house is made of brick and concrete.

INCORRECT: There house is made of brick and concrete.

INCORRECT: They're house is made of brick and concrete.

In this case, "their" is the possessive pronoun explaining to whom the house belongs.

CORRECT: He attended college with his cousins living there in California.

INCORRECT: He attended college with his cousins living their in California.

INCORRECT: He attended college with his cousins living they're in California.

"There" is referring to the state of California in the example above, so it is used to talk about the location.

CORRECT: They're away on vacation at the moment.

INCORRECT: Their away on vacation at the moment.

INCORRECT: There away on vacation at the moment.

The sentence could also be written as follows: They are away on vacation at the moment.

"They're" is a contraction of "they are," so the apostrophe needs to be used.

Correct Use of *Were*, *Where*, and *We're*:

"Were" is the past tense of the verb "are."

"Where" is used to inquire about or describe the location of something.

"We're" is a contraction of "we are."

CORRECT: They were going to call you, but the phone was out of order.

INCORRECT: They where going to call you, but the phone was out of order.

INCORRECT: They we're going to call you, but the phone was out of order.

"Were" is the past form of the verb in the sentence above.

CORRECT: Where is the mall located?

INCORRECT: Were is the mall located?

INCORRECT: We're is the mall located?

"Where" needs to be used because the sentence is making an inquiry about the location of the mall.

CORRECT: We're so happy that you got accepted into college.

INCORRECT: Were so happy that you got accepted into college.

INCORRECT: Where so happy that you got accepted into college.

The sentence could be written as follows: We are so happy that you got accepted into college.

"We're" is a contraction of "we are," so the apostrophe needs to be used.

Avoid the "is where" construction:

CORRECT: An identity crisis, which is the experience of confusion about one's life goals and ambitions, often occurs in middle age.

INCORRECT: An identity crisis is where there is the experience of confusion about one's life goals and ambitions, and it often occurs in middle age.

The construction in the second sentence may be used in informal speaking, but such constructions should be avoided in your essay.

Misplaced Modifiers:

Modifiers are phrases that describe other parts of a sentence. The modifier should always be placed directly before or after the noun to which it relates.

Now look at these examples:

CORRECT: Like Minnesota, Wisconsin gets extremely cold in the winter.

INCORRECT: Like Minnesota, it gets extremely cold in Wisconsin in the winter.

The phrase "like Minnesota" is an adjectival phrase that modifies the noun "Wisconsin."

Therefore, "Wisconsin" must come directly after the comma.

Here are two more examples:

CORRECT: While at the mall, a gang of youths committed a robbery.

INCORRECT: While at the mall, a robbery was committed.

The adverbial phrase "while at the mall" modifies the noun phrase "a gang of youths," so this noun phrase needs to come after the adverbial phrase.

Parallelism:

When giving items in a series, be sure to use consistent forms.

CORRECT: The position involves answering phone calls, writing letters, and getting supplies.

INCORRECT: The position involves answering phone calls, writing letters, and get supplies.

All of the items in the series should be in the –ing form.

CORRECT: I saw Tom's accident yesterday, and I tried to help.

INCORRECT: I saw Tom's accident yesterday, and I try to help.

Both parts of the sentence are describing actions that occurred yesterday, so the past tense (ending in –ed) needs to be used for both verbs.

Punctuation and Independent Clauses – Avoiding Run-On Sentences:

Run-on sentences are those that use commas to join independent clauses together, instead of correctly using the period.

An independent clause contains a grammatical subject and verb. It therefore can stand alone as its own sentence.

The first word of the independent clause should begin with a capital letter, and the clause should be preceded by a period.

CORRECT: I thought I would live in this city forever. Then I lost my job.

INCORRECT: I thought I would live in this city forever, then I lost my job.

"Then I lost my job" is a complete sentence. It has a grammatical subject (I) and a verb (lost). The independent clause must be preceded by a period, and the first word of the new sentence must begin with a capital letter.

Alternatively, an appropriate conjunction can be used to join the independent clauses:

I thought I would live in this city forever, and then I lost my job.

Punctuation and Quotation Marks:

Punctuation should be enclosed within the final quotation mark when giving dialogue.

CORRECT: "I can't believe you bought a new car," Sam remarked.

INCORRECT: "I can't believe you bought a new car", Sam remarked.

In the example below, the word "exclaimed" shows that the exclamation point is needed.

CORRECT: "I can't believe you bought a new car!" Sam exclaimed.

INCORRECT: "I can't believe you bought a new car"! Sam exclaimed.

However, if the quotation is stated indirectly, no quotation marks should be used.

CORRECT: Sam exclaimed that he couldn't believe that I had bought a new car.

INCORRECT: Sam exclaimed that "he couldn't believe that I had bought a new car."

Punctuation for Items in a Series:

When using "and" and "or" for more than two items in a series, be sure to use the comma before the words "and" and "or."

CORRECT: You need to bring a tent, sleeping bag, and flashlight.

INCORRECT: You need to bring a tent, sleeping bag and flashlight.

Notice the use of the comma after the word "bag" and before the word "and" in the series.

CORRECT: Students can call, write a letter, or send an email.

INCORRECT: Students can call, write a letter or send an email.

Notice the use of the comma after the word "letter" and before the word "or" in the series.

Restrictive and Non-restrictive Modifiers:

Restrictive modifiers are clauses or phrases that provide essential information in order to identify the grammatical subject. Restrictive modifiers should not be preceded by a comma.

Example: My sister who lives in Indianapolis is a good swimmer.

In this case, the speaker has more than one sister, and she is identifying which sister she is talking about by giving the essential information "who lives in Indianapolis."

On the other hand, a non-restrictive modifier is a clause or phrase that provides extra information about a grammatical subject in a sentence. A non-restrictive modifier must be preceded by a comma.

Non-restrictive modifiers are also known as non-essential modifiers.

Example: My sister, who lives in Indianapolis, is a good swimmer.

In this case, the speaker has only one sister. Therefore, the information about her sister's city of residence is not essential in order to identify which sister she is talking about.

The words "who lives in Indianapolis" form a non-restrictive modifier.

Sentence Fragments:

A sentence fragment is a group of words that does not express a complete train of thought.

CORRECT: I like Denver because it has a great university.

INCORRECT: I like Denver. Because it has a great university.

In the second example, "because it has a great university" is not a complete thought. This idea needs to be joined with the previous clause in order to be grammatically correct.

Subject-Verb Agreement:

Subjects must agree with verbs in number.

Subject-verb agreement can be confusing when there are intervening words in a sentence.

CORRECT: The flowers in the pots in the garden grow quickly.

INCORRECT: The flowers in the pots in the garden grows quickly.

The grammatical subject in the above sentence is "flowers," not "garden," so the plural form of the verb (*grow*) needs to be used.

CORRECT: Each person in the groups of students needs to pay attention to the instructions.

INCORRECT: Each person in the groups of students need to pay attention to the instructions.

The grammatical subject in the above sentence is "each person," not "students." "Each" is singular and therefore needs the singular form of the verb (*needs*).

Using Correct Grammar and Punctuation – Exercises

Each of the sentences below has problems with grammar and punctuation. Find the errors in the sentences and correct them. You may wish to refer to the advice in the previous section as you do the exercise.

The answers are provided on the page following the exercises.

1) I haven't seen her or her sister. Since they went away to college.

2) People who like to get up early in the morning in order to drink more coffee is likely to become easily tired in the afternoon.

3) Were we're you when we called you yesterday?

4) She is the most happiest person that I know.

5) Hanging from the knob on the bedroom door, Tom thought the new shirt was his favorite.

6) I ran across the street to speak to her, then she surprised me by saying "that she had bought a new car."

7) Its common for a magazine to have better sales if it mentions computers, handhelds or other new technology on it's cover.

8) After losing long-term employment, many people suffer from anxiety, loneliness and get depressed.

9) Each student in the class who will take the series of exams on advanced mathematics need to study in advance.

10) Their are several reasons why there having problems with they're children.

Using Correct Grammar and Punctuation – Answers

1) I haven't seen her or her sister since they went away to college.

2) People who like to get up early in the morning in order to drink more coffee are likely to become easily tired in the afternoon.

3) Where were you when we called you yesterday?

4) She is the happiest person that I know.

5) Hanging from the knob on the bedroom door, the new shirt was Tom's favorite.

6) I ran across the street to speak to her. Then she surprised me by saying that she had bought a new car.

7) It's common for a magazine to have better sales if it mentions computers, handhelds, or other new technology on its cover.

8) After losing long-term employment, many people suffer from anxiety, loneliness, and depression.

9) Each student in the class who will take the series of exams on advanced mathematics needs to study in advance.

10) There are several reasons why they're having problems with their children.

Sample Essays:

Look at each essay below. Then identify the thesis statement in each one. Note how each paragraph in the main body gives and elaborating idea and expands upon it. Also study the structure of the introduction and conclusion, as well as the overall structure of each essay itself. Finally, you may wish to make a note of the high-level academic vocabulary used in the essays.

Essay Question 1 – Is it ever socially acceptable to be pleased when others suffer?

While feeling pleasure when others suffer is a human emotion to which most of us would not be so quick to admit, there are occasions when it is socially acceptable to take pleasure in the pain of others. Consider, for example, the gratification that the people of European countries would have experienced when Hitler was defeated during the Second World War. Punishment for crime is another occasion where it is not considered untoward to experience satisfaction over the suffering of others. That is to say, although being pleased to see others stricken is normally not acceptable in a civilized society, there are exceptions to this general rule when others have broken the society's norms during times of war or when a criminal is to be punished for his or her wrongdoing.

Unfortunately, in modern times we have all too often seen dictators or other despotic rulers who treat the members of their societies harshly, and in such situations, the reactions of those subjected to these regimes is certainly socially justifiable. Adolph Hitler, arguably the most notorious dictator of the twentieth century, committed countless heinous acts against the inhabitants of several European countries during World War II. Due to his atrocities, previously contented residents of many towns and villages had to flee their homes in fear, leaving behind all of their worldly possessions. The most unfortunate of these persecuted individuals were submitted to unthinkable states of existence in the many death camps that Hitler oversaw. Because they were forced to live in such unimaginable conditions, those that Hitler persecuted must have been gratified when the dictator faced adversity during the war. Once Hitler had encountered the final ultimatum of surrender or death and his regime was overthrown, the relief and satisfaction openly expressed around the world on a personal level was immense.

The notion that the punishment should fit the crime is another instance of the acceptability of taking pleasure in another's suffering. Criminal law, which has been created according to traditional social convention, has been established to ensure that offenders will be justly tried and punished for their crimes. When someone has broken the norms of society in this way, other members of the community feel satisfied because they believe that justice has been served when the offender has been punished. In addition, punishing social wrongs can act as a deterrent to would-be criminals, thereby further reinforcing social norms.

Whereas taking delight in the misfortune of others is a trait that normally would not receive social approbation, the circumstances faced in war and crime fall outside this conventional social restriction. However, it is doubtful that *schadenfreude* will ever be considered a socially desirable quality outside these two situations.

Essay Question 2 – Most Americans have access to computers and cell phones on a daily basis, making email and text messaging extremely popular. While some people argue that email and texting are now the most convenient forms of personal communication, others believe that electronic communication technology is often used inappropriately. Write an essay for an audience of educated adults in which you take a position on this topic. Be sure to provide reasons and examples to support your viewpoint.

Sample Essay 2:

There is no disputing the fact that email and SMS technologies have made our lives easier in a variety of ways. Nevertheless, many of us will have had the experience of falling out with a friend or loved one over an email or text message whose content was poorly written or misconstrued. Clearly, there are certain drawbacks to emails and texts since electronic messaging cannot capture the nuances and subtleties of verbal communication. Modern forms of communication such as electronic mail and SMS messaging can cause problems with personal relationships because of three main shortcomings with these media: their impersonal nature, their inability to capture tone and sarcasm, and their easy accessibility at times of anger.

Depending upon the context, the recipient of an email or text message may consider this mode of communication to be insensitive or uncaring. Although email may be practical for conveying straightforward information or facts, electronic messaging would be remarkably inappropriate for events like announcing a death. There is no direct human contact in emails and texts, and during times of loss or tragedy, human warmth and depth of emotion can only truly be conveyed through a phone call, or better still, by talking face to face.

A further problem with emails and texts is that they do not always accurately express the tone which the writer has intended. For instance, it might be possible for the recipient of a sarcastic email message to take its contents literally. The tone of the message may seem abundantly clear to the person who sent it, but sarcastic or ironically humorous utterances can only really be communicated in speech through the tone and inflection of the voice. Without the aid of tone and inflection, certain phrases in an email may come across as demanding, indifferent, or rude.

The danger of having an accessible messaging service readily at hand during times of high emotion is another insidious problem with electronic media. In this day and age, we have heard stories not only of personal break ups that have been conducted by text, but also of employers who fire their staff by email message. Unless the writer of the message has the discipline and self-control to give him or herself a period of reasoned contemplation before sending the communication, he or she might send a regrettable message that can cause irretrievable damage to a relationship.

While email and texts may therefore be useful for certain aspects of our daily lives, these communication methods need to be handled with care in some situations, particularly when they could be seen as insensitive, when it is possible that the recipient might misinterpret the meaning, or when composed at times of personal agitation or stress. The writer of the message should use judgment and common sense in order to avoid the ill feelings that may be caused to the recipient in these cases.

ADVANTAGE+ EDITION – BONUS MATERIAL

TSI READING PRACTICE TEST 4

Instructions: Read the passages below and answer the questions that follow each one. When you have finished, you may view the answers and explanations at the end of the book.

A much-loved classic of children's literature, *Alice in Wonderland* portrays a magical world inhabited by the Mad Hatter, the Cheshire Cat, the White Rabbit, the Dormouse, and the Queen of Hearts. Based on the nursery tales that the author Lewis Carroll told to the daughter of one of his academic colleagues, the story is one part of a series that was entitled *Alice's Adventures*. The sequels, *Through the Looking Glass* and *What Alice Did Next* were also extremely popular at the time they were written. The author, whose real name was Charles Dodson, was also a gifted mathematician and enthusiastic amateur photographer.

1. The author includes the final sentence of the passage in order to:
   A. point out a lesser-known fact about the subject.
   B. state an exception to a general rule.
   C. cast doubt on a previous assertion.
   D. dispel a commonly-held falsehood.

Do mice really prefer cheese to all other foodstuffs? One well-known American exterminator has revealed his secret to catching these pesky rodents: lemon-flavored candy. It appears that the confection has a double advantage. Its sweet smells attracts the mouse much more strongly than does cheese, and its sticky consistency helps to hold the creature captive for the moment it takes for the trap to release. Through logical analogy, we can therefore conclude that it is fallacious to presume that other groups of animals have preferences for certain food groups. For instance, we cannot readily conclude that all dogs would choose meat or that all cats would select milk as their favorite foodstuffs.

2. Which of the following, if true, would most strongly suggest that the logical analogy mentioned in the passage is incorrect?
   A. Mice are attracted more to the texture of the candy than to its smell.
   B. Some animals have a very acute sense of smell.
   C. Many scientific experiments demonstrate that dogs do not prefer the taste and texture of meat to the taste and texture of other food.
   D. Independent observations reveal that mice eat cheese as often as they lemon-flavored candy when both foodstuffs are available to them at the same time.

Ludwig von Beethoven was one of the most influential figures in the development of musical forms during the Classical period. Born in Bonn, Germany, the composer became a professional musician before the age of 12. After studying under both Mozart and Haydn, Beethoven became a virtuoso pianist and had many wealthy patrons, who supported him financially. His most popular works are considered to be his fifth and sixth symphonies, and his only opera is entitled *Fidelio*. It is generally agreed that his compositions express the creative energy of the artist himself, rather than being written to suit the demands of his patrons.

3.   The primary purpose of the passage is to:
   A. suggest that the works of Beethoven, Mozart, and Haydn are very similar.
   B. explore the development of musical composition during the Classical period.
   C. provide background information about Beethoven's life and work.
   D. explain how Beethoven acquired many wealthy patrons.

Painted by the Norwegian artist Edvard Munch, *The Scream* depicts the skeletal face of a person in clear psychological distress. Contrasted against a serene background of asymmetrical red and yellow swirls that represent the sunset, the desperation in the facial characteristics of the subject is said to express humanity's reaction to the anxieties of modern life. Completing the work at the age of 29, Munch admitted that he felt as if a scream went through himself during that time since he was in a state of poor mental and physical health while painting the piece.

4.   According to the passage, which one of the following factors most influenced Munch's painting of *The Scream*?
   A. his age at the time of working on the painting
   B. his own lack of psychological and physiological well-being
   C. humanity's experiences of the anxieties of modern life
   D. the colors of the sunset

Today archaeologists are still endeavoring to uncover the secrets of Africa's past. Even though the artifacts and skeletons of early Africans are most commonly found in a highly fragmented state, these findings are more than sufficient in order to make a number of significant conclusions. Perhaps the most important discovery is that there is great *variation* among the human remains, indicating a wide array of physical differences among members of the population. While the early population was diverse, it has been well established that the earliest species of hominids spread from Africa to other continents. The first traces of human technology, consisting of simple stone tools, were also discovered in Africa. Having been developed long before the invention of metallurgy, tools had gradually become smaller and more sophisticated. Microliths, fine stone tools that were fitted to handles, were used as cutting and scraping tools and may even have been the precursor to the bow and arrow.

5.	From the passage, it can be inferred that some of the archeological discoveries from Africa:
	A.	were broken into small pieces or extremely damaged.
	B.	would not have been located without modern genetic science.
	C.	were not as important as those from other continents.
	D.	supported the development of metallurgy.

Known as the Centennial State, Colorado is divided into sixty-three counties. The eastern part of the state was gained by the U.S. in 1803 as part of the Louisiana Purchase, while the western part was acquired from Mexico by treaty in 1848. Colorado joined the union as the 38th state in 1876, shortly after the first substantial discovery of gold in the state near Pikes Peak in 1859. The Rocky Mountains run along a north-south line through the center of the state, and there are several famous national parks and monuments, including Rocky Mountain National Park, Black Canyon of the Gunnison National Park, Mesa Verde, Dinosaur National Monument, and the Great Sand Dunes National Monument. Agriculture in the state involves the production of wheat, hay, corn, sugar beets, and other crops, as well as cattle ranching and raising other livestock. The packaging, processing, fabrication, and defense industries form the *lion's share of* revenues from business and commerce in the state. Perhaps lesser-known is the fact that Colorado contains the world's largest deposits of molybdenum, a brittle silver-grey metallic chemical element that is used in some alloy steels.

6.	The primary purpose of the passage is to:
	A.	discuss trade and commerce in a particular state.
	B.	sum up the historical background and notable features of a particular state.
	C.	provide pertinent political details about the acquisition of a particular state.
	D.	emphasize the importance of agriculture for trade and commerce in Colorado.

Depicting the events of a single day, James Joyce's epic novel *Ulysses* took more than 20,000 hours, or a total of eight years, to write. Set in Dublin, the novel was initially published in installments as a series before the Parisian publishing house Shakespeare and Company issued a limited edition of 1,000 copies. The book was risqué for its time, and was classified as obscene material in the United Stated. After the work was cleared of obscenity charges, an unexpurgated version was accepted for publication by Random House in New York. Ironically, it was not available in Dublin until 40 years later.

7.	The author suggests which of the following about the fact that *Ulysses* was published in Dublin 40 years after it was released in New York?
	A.	Irish publishing companies often engage in dilatory practices when dealing with their authors.
	B.	Irish publishers were dissuaded in publishing the novel since it depicted the events of only one day.
	C.	Random House did not have a division in Dublin at that time.
	D.	Social mores in Dublin were much stricter than those of the United States at that time.

A complex series of interactive patterns govern nearly everything the human body does. We eat to a rhythm and drink, sleep, and even breathe to separate ones. Research shows that the human body clock is affected by three main rhythmic cycles: the rhythm at which the earth revolves on its axis, the monthly revolution of the moon around the earth, and the annual revolution of the earth around the sun. These rhythms create a sense of time that is both physiological as well as mental. Humans feel hungry about every four hours, sleep about eight hours in every 24-hour period, and dream in cycles of approximately 90 minutes each. These natural rhythms, sometimes called circadian rhythms, are partially controlled by the hypothalamus in the brain. Circadian rhythms help to explain the "lark vs. owl" hypothesis. Larks are those who quite rightly prefer to rise early in the morning and go to bed early, while owls are those who feel at their best at night and stay up too late. These cycles explain the phenomenon of jet lag, when the individual's body clock is out of step with the actual clock time in his or her new location in the world. In humans, births and deaths also follow predictable cycles, with most births and deaths occurring at night.

8. The author's attitude toward owls in the "lark vs. owl" hypothesis can best be described as one of:
    A. disapproval
    B. skepticism
    C. hostility
    D. support

Gibberellins are a complex group of plant hormones that are involved in many botanical processes. Commonly used in combination with similar botanical hormones called auxins, their primary function is to promote plant growth by controlling the elongation of cells. They also promote the formation of fruit and seed, as well as delay aging in leaves. Having become important for commercial reasons in recent years, the hormones are also used to help meet the ever-growing demand for new hybrids of plants and flowers.

9. Which of the following best describes the botanical significance of gibberellins?
    A. Without them, plant hormones would be involved in more processes.
    B. Because of gibberellins, plant cells enlarge, thereby causing plants to grow.
    C. Leaves age more quickly, owing to the function of gibberellins.
    D. Gibberellins have nocuous consequences for fruits and seeds.

For every building that is successfully constructed, there are countless others that have never received the chance to leave the drawing board. Some of these unbuilt structures were practical and mundane, while others expressed the flights of fancy of the architect. Known to us today only through the plans left on paper, many unbuilt buildings were originally designed to commemorate particular people or events. Such was the case with the monument dubbed the *Beacon of Progress*, which was to be erected in Chicago to display exhibits dedicated to great Americans in history. However, scholar Samantha Mulholland points out that other proposed projects were far more quixotic, like that of *The Floating Spheres*, described as modules held aloft by hot air to house cities of the future.

10. Samantha Mulholland suggests that which of the following explains why some proposed projects were never constructed?
    A. Some projects were never undertaken due to the fact that they did not commemorate any significant event.
    B. The plans for some projects had serious design flaws.
    C. Some projects were too extravagant and impractical ever to be built.
    D. People were not ready to face the future of housing at the time that the construction of *The Floating Spheres* was proposed.

The ancient legal code of Babylonia had severe sanctions for a wide range of crimes. Perhaps best viewed as a way to express personal vengeance, punishments included cutting off the fingers of boys who had hit their fathers or gouging out the eyes of those who had blinded another person. As with most ancient peoples, the Babylonians did not believe in humane treatments for offenders. Sumerian King Ur Nammu, who formulated a set of laws that were surprisingly modern in their approach, did not follow these draconian forms of retribution. Sumerian law stipulated that perpetrators of violent crimes pay monetary damages to their victims, and Ur Nammu's system is the first recorded example of financial awards being imposed in lieu of other forms of punishment.

11. The author mentions Sumerian King Ur Nammu primarily in order to:
    A. criticize previous Babylonian rulers.
    B. emphasize the severity of the Babylonian system of justice.
    C. imply that Babylonian sanctions were just for their time.
    D. provide a contrast with the forms of punishment meted out by the Babylonians.

Educational psychology studies pupils in a classroom setting in order to help educators to understand the behaviors and attitudes that affect learning and teaching. This branch of psychology was a reaction against the psychometric movement, which tested students in order to place them into "streamed" classes of different ability levels. The popularity of IQ testing and streamed education declined in the second half of the twentieth century, and the education profession is now focused on developing programs that view students as individuals and advising schools how better to function as organizations.

12. According to the passage, the best way to distinguish between the education profession before the second half of the twentieth century and current educational practice would be by:
    A. looking at the results of psychometric testing.
    B. studying pupils in a classroom setting.
    C. supporting the benefits of IQ testing.
    D. determining whether students are grouped into categories based on test results.

Born Marguerite Johnson, Maya Angelou was an American writer, poet, educator, and actor. Her seven autobiographies, based on her experiences of childhood and as a young adult, have been published around the world and have received international acclaim. From her writings, we know that Angelou was abused as a child and had a baby at sixteen, before going on to work as an actress and school administrator. Her writings are widely regarded as celebrating the African-American experience, as well as the capacity not only to survive hardship, but also to thrive and flourish in the face of adversity.

13. The author mentions Angelou's childhood abuse most likely in order to:
     A. give an example of the hardship that she faced.
     B. provide a contrast to her work as a school administrator.
     C. reveal the main basis of her autobiographical writing.
     D. suggest the reason why she did not write under her real name.

Although the foundations of the movement can be traced back to the artists van Gogh and Gauguin in the late nineteenth century, the first recorded use of the term Expressionism was in Germany in the early twentieth century. Influencing art, literature, theater, and architecture, Expressionism strives to illustrate the inner emotional reaction to a reality. In this approach, the traditional notion of realism is to be disregarded, as are the conventional ideas of beauty and proportion. Accordingly, Expressionist artists use distortion, incongruous color schemes, and exaggerated shapes and sizes to reveal their emotions. The impact of the movement is also present in fictional and poetic works of the era, particularly those which represent the dislocation of the individual within society.

14. The passage suggests that Expressionism illustrates which one of the following phenomena?
     A. Artistic movements are ever-changing with the passage of time.
     B. Abstract art is more popular than realistic art.
     C. Human beings felt out of sync with their communities at the time this movement was taking place.
     D. Most twentieth century artists were nonconventional.

The Higgs mechanism is the process in quantum field theory whereby symmetry is broken down, leading to massive particles. Quantum field theory alone tells us that all particles should be massless. Yet, groundbreaking scientific research has found that particles can acquire mass when the symmetry of energy within a system is less than that of the interaction governing the system. Theoretically, scientists understand that the Higgs particle is a by-product of the acquisition of mass by other particles. Discovering this elusive particle remains one of the greatest challenges of modern-day particle physicists.

15. The author most likely elaborates on quantum field theory in the second sentence in order to:
     A. change the subject from mechanisms to particles.
     B. reveal that the Higgs mechanism inheres in a basic contradiction.
     C. illustrate how the symmetry of energy within a system can be lower than that of the governing system.
     D. explain the process by which massive particles are formed.

118

Recent research shows that interaction with flowers and other botanicals has many benefits for our health. In fact, several recent studies link floral products with human well-being. Flower arranging not only combines lovely aromas with beautiful colors and textures, but also makes a person feel closer to nature. In addition, floral design is a creative and calming activity that challenges the mind, requiring its participants to focus on visual skills that improve cognition, information processing, and memory. Another study found that the mere presence of flowers has an immediate effect on mood and happiness. Those in the study who had frequent contact with an environment that had flowers reported more positive moods and less anxiety. Notably, flowers appeared to have the most positive impact upon seniors, reducing depression and encouraging interaction with others. These beautiful plants help employees to have more enthusiasm and energy at work as well, leading to innovative thinking and more original solutions. Studies like these seem to confirm what I have always known instinctively: that having flowers makes us feel better in many ways.

16.   Why is floral design good for the mind?
       A. It has nice aromas, colors, and textures.
       B. People feel relaxed because they are close to nature.
       C. People have to visualize and think about how to organize the flowers.
       D. It makes its participants happy and in a better mood than before.

Studies of the human body show that performance ability can be enhanced by regular strenuous training exercises. Some human athletic records may seem unbeatable, but these achievements require great effort. When compared to the innate abilities of animals, the athletic training and performance of human beings seem unimpressive, paling in comparison to the phenomenal feats performed naturally by members of the animal kingdom. Whales, for example, usually dive to 3,700 feet below sea level. However, the human body can withstand underwater depths up to only 2,300 feet, and attempting to do so requires special equipment. Human performance also seems paltry in swimming when compared to other species. The human record for the fastest swimming speed is 5.3 miles per hour. However, the sailfish averages a speed of 68 miles per hour, and the penguin, which is not even a member of the fish species, can flutter across the surface of the water as fast as 22 miles per hour.

17.   What is the main idea of the passage?
       A. The human body needs training in order to compete in athletic events.
       B. Fish can swim far better than human beings.
       C. Fish can go deeper under water than humans can.
       D. The athletic performance of some animals is superior to that of humans.

Recent studies show that coffee may be even worse for us than we thought. We have known for a few years now that coffee can elevate blood pressure and also lead to high cholesterol, but new research has revealed a whole host of other health problems caused by the beverage. A new study demonstrates that coffee stimulates the secretion of gastric acid, which can lead to stomach upset. So, if you frequently suffer from stomach ache, it would be a good idea to cut down on coffee or stop drinking it altogether. Consuming coffee later in the day is strongly linked to insomnia, which can cause health problems like anxiety and depression. Caffeine stays in your system for six hours, so don't have coffee after 2:00 pm unless you drink decaffeinated. A further study has shown that coffee changes our sense of taste, making sweet things seem less sweet. This may cause us to crave more sweets. However, avoid adding sugar, cream, or milk to your coffee. With raised calorie levels, continued consumption of such sugar-laden beverages can lead to obesity and type-two diabetes.

18.   According to the passage, how can coffee cause stomach ache?
        A. Drinking too much of it fills up the stomach.
        B. The caffeine in the beverage irritates the stomach.
        C. It makes acidity levels in the stomach higher.
        D. Stomach ache is linked to adding too much sugar.

In his book *Il Milione*, known in English as *The Travels of Marco Polo*, the intrepid explorer describes the marvels he encountered as he journeyed to China. Upon his visit to the emperor Kublai Khan in Cathay, Polo witnessed the magical illusions performed by the court wizards of the supreme ruler. Watching in amazement as the wizards recited incantations, Polo first saw a row of golden cups *levitate* over the table as Khan drank from each one without spilling a drop. Polo also recounted that Khan had astonishing powers over wild animals. Unrestrained and ostensibly obedient, lions would appear to lie down in humility in front of the emperor.

However, Khan was venerated for much more than these acts of mere wizardry. Polo's account tells us that the ruler presided over an extremely modern state. Paper currency, integrated with seals of authenticity to prevent counterfeiting, existed during Khan's rule. In addition, his establishment of a vast postal system meant that he would receive news in a fraction of the time that was normally required. Under the rule of Khan, the roads of the empire were also well-maintained, and travelers could reach their destinations relatively quickly and efficiently. Although some academics have disputed the veracity of Polo's written account of the Khan Empire, common sense tells us that there would have been little motive for the explorer to have exaggerated his version of events since he was being held captive at the time with no hope of release.

19.   It can be inferred from the passage that the primary reason why the court wizards performed magical illusions was to:
        A. venerate the majesty of Kublai Khan.
        B. play a trick on Marco Polo.
        C. provide an interesting story for the book *Il Milione*.
        D. make Kublai Khan and his court appear powerful and mysterious.

20. The author most probably uses the word "levitate" in paragraph 1 to mean:
A. rise
B. drag
C. hover
D. linger

21. Some academics find fault with *Il Milione* for its failure to answer which of the following questions:
A. Why does Marco Polo's account go against common sense?
B. Did paper currency really exist during Khan's rule?
C. Was Khan's state as modern as Polo described?
D. Why should we believe Polo's version of events?

22. Which of the following best describes the organization of the passage?
A. It gives the historical background to a piece of writing and then provides further details about it.
B. It recounts a story and then offers an explanation.
C. It describes a social phenomenon and then illustrates it.
D. It compares one version of a historical event to a differing account and interpretation of the event.

In my opinion, only two significant original forms of theater have emerged from Japanese culture: Noh and Kabuki. Noh, the older form, was originally established to meet the demands of the "discriminating Japanese aristocracy" and remained "unchanged for more than six centuries." Noh renders mundane, everyday activities, like drinking tea or arranging flowers, into exquisite artistic performances. Consisting of minimal spectacle, bare stage designs, and little spoken dialogue, Noh is classified as more ritual than drama. In order to convey the dialogue, a chorus sings the protagonist's lines while the performer engages in the "solemn act" of the dance.

Kabuki performances are discernably different than those of Noh. Based on puppet theater, Kabuki is designed to meet the tastes of the general populace, rather than those of the aristocracy. According to long-standing theatrical custom, Kabuki performances can be extremely long, lasting up to twelve hours in some cases. Since movement plays a greater role than dialogue, Kabuki actors must wear heavy makeup and engage in highly stylized actions. Because of its appeal to the general populace, Kabuki theater remains as fascinating and exotic as it has always been, even though its purity has been somewhat compromised through exposure to other cultures.

23. The author's use of quotations in the passage suggests which of the following about followers of Noh?
A. The followers of Noh are traditional, discerning, and serious.
B. They believe that Kabuki theater is overtly flamboyant.
C. They fear that the popularity of Kabuki theater may diminish the appeal of Noh.
D. They plan to make Noh more up-to-date in order to increase its following.

24. The second paragraph implies that Japanese audiences today would respond to Kabuki theater with:
   A. admiration
   B. impatience
   C. confusion
   D. boredom

25. Followers of Noh and followers of Kabuki would probably agree with which one of the following statements?
   A. Theatrical productions sometimes last too long.
   B. Japanese theater is unlikely to change in the future.
   C. The purity of all forms of Japanese theater has been compromised through exposure to other cultures.
   D. Japanese theater is an important and interesting aspect of Japanese culture.

ANSWERS TO TSI READING PRACTICE TEST 4

1.   The correct answer is A. The final sentence of the passage is as follows: "The author, whose real name was Charles Dodson, was also a gifted mathematician and enthusiastic amateur photographer." The author includes the final sentence of the passage in order to point out a lesser-known fact about the subject. Many people will know that Lewis Carroll is the author of *Alice in Wonderland.* However, they may not know Lewis Carroll's real name or his other skills.

2.   The correct answer is D. The passage states: "Through logical analogy, we can therefore conclude that it is fallacious to presume that other groups of animals have preferences for certain food groups." The logical analogy mentioned in the passage would be incorrect if it were true that mice eat cheese as often as they lemon-flavored candy when both foodstuffs are available to them at the same time. If the mice eat both food groups equally, they would not have a preference, and the logical analogy relies upon the existence of this preference.

3.   The correct answer is C. The primary purpose of the passage is to provide background information about Beethoven's life and work. The passage begins by providing information about the composer's musical training, before going on to talk about his professional life and compositions.

4.   The correct answer is B. Munch's own lack of psychological and physiological well-being most influenced his painting of *The Scream*. The last sentence of the passage explains that "Munch admitted that he felt as if a scream went through himself during that time since he was in a state of poor mental and physical health while painting the piece." Note that "physiological" and "physical" are synonyms.

5.   The correct answer is A. From the passage, it can be inferred that some of the archeological discoveries from Africa were broken into small pieces or extremely damaged. The last sentence of paragraph 1 of the passage tells us that "the artifacts and skeletons of early Africans are most commonly found in a highly fragmented state." "Fragmented" means broken into pieces.

6.   The correct answer is B. The primary purpose of the passage is to sum up the historical background and notable features of a particular state. The other answer choices provide specific details from the passage, rather than the primary purpose.

7.   The correct answer is D. The author suggests that social mores in Dublin were much stricter than those of the United States at the time that *Ulysses* was published in New York. The passage tells us that "the book was risqué for its time" and was originally classified as "obscene material." In this context, the word "mores" means moral views, and the word "risqué" means indecent.

8.   The correct answer is A. The author's attitude toward owls in the "lark vs. owl" hypothesis can best be described as one of disapproval. The author says that larks "quite rightly prefer to rise early in the morning," but owls "stay up too late." So, the author disapproves of the owl's behavior.

9.   The correct answer is B. Gibberellins are of botanical significance because they cause plant cells to enlarge, thereby causing plants to grow. The passage states that the primary function of gibberellins "is to promote plant growth by controlling the elongation of cells."

10.   The correct answer is C. Samantha Mulholland suggests some proposed projects were never constructed because they were too extravagant and impractical ever to be built. The passage states: "Scholar Samantha Mulholland points out other proposed projects were far more quixotic." The word "quixotic" means extravagant and impractical.

11.   The correct answer is D. The author mentions Sumerian King Ur Nammu primarily in order to provide a contrast with the usual forms of punishment meted out by the Babylonians. The passage states that "the Babylonians did not believe in humane treatments for offenders." However, King Ur Nammu "did not follow these draconian forms of retribution."

12.   The correct answer is D. According to the passage, the best way to distinguish between the education profession before the second half of the twentieth century and current educational practice is by determining whether students are grouped into categories based on test results. The passage explains that students used to be placed "into 'streamed' classes of different ability levels." However, current educational practice is to "view students as individuals."

13.   The correct answer is A. The author mentions Angelou's childhood abuse most likely in order to give an example of the hardship that she faced. After mentioning the examples from Angelou's life, the passage explains that "Her writings are widely regarded as celebrating the African-American experience, as well as the capacity [. . .] to survive hardship."

14.   The correct answer is C. The passage suggests that Expressionism illustrates the way in which human beings felt out of sync with their communities at the time this movement was taking place. The last sentence of the passage comments that Expressionism represents "the dislocation of the individual within society."

15.   The correct answer is B. The author most likely mentions quantum field theory in order to reveal that the Higgs mechanism inheres in a basic contradiction. In other words, quantum field theory tells us that all particles should be massless, but the Higgs mechanism shows that particles can acquire mass.

16.   The correct answer is C. Floral design is good for the mind because people have to visualize and think about how to organize the flowers. The text explains that floral design requires "its participants to focus on visual skills." Notice that the question is asking about floral design in particular, rather than flowers in general.

17.   The correct answer is D. The main idea of the passage is that the athletic performance of some animals is superior to that of humans. The text states: "the athletic training and performance of human beings seem unimpressive, paling in comparison to the phenomenal feats performed naturally by members of the animal kingdom."

18.   The correct answer is C. Coffee can cause stomach ache because it makes acidity levels in the stomach higher. The text explains that "coffee stimulates the secretion of gastric acid, which can lead to stomach upset."

19.   The correct answer is D. It can be inferred from the passage that the primary reason why the court wizards performed magical illusions was to make Kublai Khan and his court appear powerful and mysterious. The first paragraph uses the words "amazement" and "astonishing" to express the mysteriousness of the court.

20.   The correct answer is C. The author most probably uses the word "levitate" in paragraph 1 to mean hover. The words "levitate" and "hover" both mean to be suspended in midair.

21.   The correct answer is D. Some academics find fault with *Il Milione* for its failure to answer the following question: Why should we believe Polo's version of events? The passage explains that "Although some academics have disputed the veracity of Polo's written account of the Khan Empire, common sense tells us that there would have been little motive for the explorer to have exaggerated his version of events." The phrase "dispute the veracity" means that they doubt whether the story is true.

22.   The correct answer is A. The passage gives the historical background to a piece of writing and then provides further details about it. Paragraph 1 describes the book *Il Milione*, and paragraph 2 provides some additional information about Polo's written account of events.

23.   The correct answer is A. The use of quotations in the passage suggests that the followers of Noh are traditional, discerning, and serious. Paragraph 1 uses quotation marks when it states that Noh is for the "discriminating Japanese aristocracy" and that it depicts a "solemn act." The word "aristocracy" indicates that the dance is traditional in nature. "Discriminating" means "discerning," and "solemn" means "serious."

24.   The correct answer is A. The second paragraph implies that Japanese audiences today would respond to Kabuki theater with admiration. The last sentence of the second paragraph states: "Because of its appeal to the general populace, Kabuki theater

remains as fascinating and exotic as it has always been." We can surmise that people probably admire something that fascinates them.

25.   The correct answer is D. Followers of Noh and followers of Kabuki would probably agree that Japanese theater is an important and interesting aspect of Japanese culture. The first sentence of the passage explains that these forms of theater "have emerged from Japanese culture." Since an article has been devoted to this topic, we can assume that followers consider the topic to be an important and interesting aspect of the Japanese culture.

ESSAY CORRECTION EXERCISES

Instructions: The draft essays below contain errors. Choose the correct version of each part of each sentence from the answer choices provided. If the part of the sentence is correct as written, you should choose answer A. The answers are given at the end of the exercises.

Essay 1 – The Philosophy of Human Nature

[1] The study of the philosophy of human nature is often regarded as an investigation at the meaning of life. [2] This subject deals with four key problem areas: human choice, human thought, human personality, and the unity of the human being. [3] A consideration in these four problem areas [4] can include scientific also and artistic viewpoints on the nature of human life.

[5] The first problem area human choice, asks [6] whether human beings can really make decisions that can change their futures. [7] However, it investigates to what extent the individual's future is fixed [8] and pre-determined then cosmic forces outside the control of human beings.

[9] In the second problem area, human thought, epistemology is considering. [10] Epistemology means the study of knowledge, it should not be confused with ontology, the study of being or existence

[11] The third key issue, human personality, emphasized aspects of human life that are beyond mental processes. [12] They takes a look at emotional, spiritual, and communal elements. [13] Important, the study of the communal aspect focuses on community and communication, [14] instead on government or the philosophy of the state.

[15] Finally, the fourth problem, the unity of the human being, explores the first three areas more full [16] and asks if that there is any unifying basis for human choice, thought, and

127

personality. [17] In other words, while the human is an inherently complex being, there must be a unity or wholeness which underlies these complications.

[18] The study of the philosophy of human nature can be enable an individual to contemplate more deeply vital human issues, [19] included an engagement with political, cultural, and social debates. [20] Not surprisingly, the works of Plato and Aristotle is generally regarded as the foundation for this subject.

Item 1.

    A.   The study of the philosophy of human nature is often regarded as an investigation at the meaning of life.

    B.   The study of the philosophy of human nature is often regarded as an investigation for the meaning of life.

    C.   The study of the philosophy of human nature is often regarded as an investigation about the meaning of life.

    D.   The study of the philosophy of human nature is often regarded as an investigation into the meaning of life.

Item 2.

    A.   This subject deals with four key problem areas: human choice, human thought, human personality, and the unity of the human being.

    B.   This subject deals with four key problem areas, human choice, human thought, human personality, and the unity of the human being.

    C.   This subject deals with four key problem areas; human choice, human thought, human personality, and the unity of the human being.

    D.   This subject deals with four key problem areas. Human choice, human thought, human personality, and the unity of the human being.

Item 3.

    A.   A consideration in these four problem areas

    B.   A consideration with these four problem areas

C. A consideration for these four problem areas

D. A consideration of these four problem areas

Item 4.

A. can include scientific also and artistic viewpoints on the nature of human life.

B. can include scientific and artistic viewpoints also on the nature of human life.

C. can also include scientific and artistic viewpoints on the nature of human life.

D. can include scientific and artistic viewpoints on also the nature of human life.

Item 5.

A. The first problem area human choice, asks

B. The first problem area, human choice, asks

C. The first, problem area, human choice, asks

D. The first problem area human choice asks,

Item 6.

A. whether human beings can really make decisions that can change their futures.

B. whether human beings can really make decisions that can change his futures.

C. whether human beings can really make decisions that can change its futures.

D. whether human beings can really make decisions that can change one's future.

Item 7.

A. However, it investigates to what extent the individual's future is fixed

B. Conversely, it investigates to what extent the individual's future is fixed

C. Negatively, it investigates to what extent the individual's future is fixed

D. Despite, it investigates to what extent the individual's future is fixed

Item 8.

A. and pre-determined then cosmic forces outside the control of human beings.

B. and pre-determined according cosmic forces outside the control of human beings.

C. and pre-determined by cosmic forces outside the control of human beings.

D. and pre-determined after cosmic forces outside the control of human beings.

Item 9.

    A.   In the second problem area, human thought, epistemology is considering.

    B.   In the second problem area, human thought, epistemology considering.

    C.   In the second problem area, human thought, epistemology is considered.

    D.   In the second problem area, human thought, epistemology being considered.

Item 10.

    A.   Epistemology means the study of knowledge, it should not be confused with ontology, the study of being or existence.

    B.   Epistemology means the study of knowledge: it should not be confused with ontology, the study of being or existence.

    C.   Epistemology means the study of knowledge; it should not be confused with ontology, the study of being or existence.

    D.   Epistemology means the study of knowledge, which it should not be confused with ontology, the study of being or existence.

Item 11.

    A.   The third key issue, human personality, emphasized aspects of human life that are beyond mental processes.

    B.   The third key issue, human personality, had emphasized aspects of human life that are beyond mental processes.

    C.   The third key issue, human personality, is emphasizing aspects of human life that are beyond mental processes.

    D.   The third key issue, human personality, emphasizes aspects of human life that are beyond mental processes.

Item 12.

    A.   They takes a look at emotional, spiritual, and communal elements.

    B.   One take at a look at emotional, spiritual, and communal elements.

    C.   You take a look at emotional, spiritual, and communal elements.

    D.   It takes a look at emotional, spiritual, and communal elements.

Item 13.
- A. Important, the study of the communal aspect focuses on community and communication,
- B. Importantly, the study of the communal aspect focuses on community and communication,
- C. The importantly study of the communal aspect focuses on community and communication,
- D. The study of the importantly communal aspect focuses on community and communication,

Item 14.
- A. instead on government or the philosophy of the state.
- B. rather on government or the philosophy of the state.
- C. rather than on government or the philosophy of the state.
- D. beside that on government or the philosophy of the state.

Item 15.
- A. Finally, the fourth problem, the unity of the human being, explores the first three areas more full
- B. Finally, the fourth problem, the unity of the human being, explores the first three areas more fully
- C. Finally, the fourth problem, the unity of the human being, explores the first more fully three areas
- D. Finally, the fourth problem, the unity of the human being, explores the first more full three areas

Item 16.
- A. and asks if that there is any unifying basis for human choice, thought, and personality.
- B. and asks if is any unifying basis for human choice, thought, and personality.
- C. and asks whether there is any unifying basis for human choice, thought, and personality.

D. and asks whether is there any unifying basis for human choice, thought, and personality.

Item 17.

    A. In other words, while the human is an inherently complex being, there must be a unity or wholeness which underlies these complications.

    B. In other words, while the human is an inherently complex being, there must be a unity or wholeness which underlied these complications.

    C. In other words, while the human is an inherently complex being, there must be a unity or wholeness that underlying these complications.

    D. In other words, while the human is an inherently complex being, there must be a unity or wholeness whose underlying these complications.

Item 18.

    A. The study of the philosophy of human nature can be enable an individual to contemplate more deeply vital human issues,

    B. The study of the philosophy of human nature can be enabled an individual to contemplate more deeply vital human issues,

    C. The study of the philosophy of human nature should be enable an individual to contemplate more deeply vital human issues,

    D. The study of the philosophy of human nature should enable an individual to contemplate more deeply vital human issues,

Item 19.

    A. included an engagement with political, cultural, and social debates.

    B. including an engagement with political, cultural, and social debates.

    C. inclusive an engagement with political, cultural, and social debates.

    D. inclusion of an engagement with political, cultural, and social debates.

Item 20.

    A.   Not surprisingly, the works of Plato and Aristotle is generally regarded as the foundation for this subject.

    B.   Not surprisingly, the works of Plato and Aristotle are generally regarded as the foundation for this subject.

    C.   Not surprisingly, the works of Plato and Aristotle is regarded generally as the foundation for this subject.

    D.   Not surprisingly, the works of Plato and Aristotle were generally regarded as the foundation for this subject.

Item 21.

Imagine that the student wanted to add a sentence to the second paragraph emphasizing the reasons for the importance of human choice. Which of the following sentences accomplishes this?

    A.   A sense of control over one's life is also extremely important.

    B.   Feeling in control of one's life is important for those who believe in destiny.

    C.   Feelings of individual control support the belief in chance, fate, and destiny.

    D.   A sense of control over one's life can enable an individual to make empowering decisions about his or her future.

Item 22.

If the student were to eliminate the last paragraph of the essay, the essay would lack

    A.   an explanation of the outcome of the study of philosophy.

    B.   an insight into the attitudes of some of the world's most important philosophers.

    C.   the inference that philosophy is an abstruse subject.

    D.   the recommendation of which books a student of philosophy should read.

Essay 2 – The Middle Ages

[1] The Middle Ages period were a time of significant social and political change. [2] Even though the Germanic invasion in the fifth century, [3] the autocratic system of Roman government had overthrown. [4] In that place today is a collection of independent democratic nations. [5] However, this development would not have been possible whether its foundations had not been laid throughout the Middle Ages.

[6] Indeed, a productive process lay beneath many seemingly everyday, bantering activities during this era. [7] New societies began to materialize as for the German invaders became acquainted with the Roman inhabitants. [8] This intermingling of nationalities and ethnic groups was an important process, that should not be overlooked [9] because those type of hybridity bears [10] a great deal of resemblance with the ethnic diversity of certain communities in modern society.

[11] Nevertheless, economic layers was still present at this time. [12] Many of the warriors invading had established themselves as affluent farmers. [13] It's wealth was in stark contrast to the life of the lower class slaves and peasants, [14] who often had large families.

[15] In addition, this period witnessed the rise in imperialism, defined as a political system for which a king or queen has absolute power. [16] While many kings strived to rule in accordance with the law, some rulers treated their citizens harshly, without establishing followed legal restrictions.

[17] Yet, their appalling living conditions, the common populace began to challenge the imperial system during the Middle Ages. [18] Changing the attitudes of people towards their

rulers, [19] the balance of power in the political system also began to have shift. [20] To a significant extent, these challenges influenced the functioning of present-day political systems.

Item 1.

A.   The Middle Ages period were a time of significant social and political change.

B.   The Middle Ages period was a time of significant social and political change.

C.   The Middle Age's period were a time of significant social and political change.

D.   The Middle Age's period was a time of significant social and political change.

Item 2.

A.   Even though the Germanic invasion in the fifth century,

B.   Despite of the Germanic invasion in the fifth century,

C.   As a result of the Germanic invasion in the fifth century,

D.   In effect, the Germanic invasion in the fifth century,

Item 3.

A.   the autocratic system of Roman government had overthrown.

B.   the autocratic system of Roman government have overthrown.

C.   the autocratic system of Roman government to have overthrown.

D.   the autocratic system of Roman government was overthrown.

Item 4.

A.   In that place today is a collection of independent democratic nations.

B.   In it's place today is a collection of independent democratic nations.

C.   In its place today is a collection of independent democratic nations.

D.   In one's place today is a collection of independent democratic nations.

Item 5.

A.   However, this development would not have been possible whether its foundations had not been laid throughout the Middle Ages.

B.   However, this development would not have been possible whether its foundations were not been lain throughout the Middle Ages.

C.   However, this development would not have been possible if it's foundations were not layed throughout the Middle Ages.

D.   However, this development would not have been possible if its foundations had not been laid throughout the Middle Ages.

Item 6.

A.   Indeed, a productive process lay beneath many seemingly everyday, bantering activities during this era.

B.   Indeed, a productive process lay beneath many seemingly everyday, benign activities during this era.

C.   Indeed, a productive process lay beneath many seemingly everyday, bogus activities during this era.

D.   Indeed, a productive process lay beneath many seemingly everyday, banal activities during this era.

Item 7.

A.   New societies began to materialize as for the German invaders became acquainted with the Roman inhabitants.

B.   New societies began to materialize as when the German invaders became acquainted with the Roman inhabitants.

C.   New societies began to materialize as while the German invaders became acquainted with the Roman inhabitants.

D.   New societies began to materialize as the German invaders became acquainted with the Roman inhabitants.

Item 8.

A.   This intermingling of nationalities and ethnic groups was an important process, that should not be overlooked

B.   This intermingling of nationalities and ethnic groups was an important process. That should not be overlooked

C.   This intermingling of nationalities and ethnic groups was an important process that should not be overlooked

D.   This intermingling of nationalities and ethnic groups was an important process, one should not be overlooked

Item 9.
A.   because those type of hybridity bears
B.   because these type of hybridity bears
C.   because this type of hybridity bears
D.   because that types of hybridity bears

Item 10.
A.   a great deal of resemblance with the ethnic diversity of certain communities in modern society.
B.   a great deal of resemblance to the ethnic diversity of certain communities in modern society.
C.   a great deal of resemblance like the ethnic diversity of certain communities in modern society.
D.   a great deal of resemblance such as to the ethnic diversity of certain communities in modern society.

Item 11.
A.   Nevertheless, economic layers was still present at this time.
B.   Nevertheless, economic stratification was still present at this time.
C.   Nevertheless, economic strata was still present at this time.
D.   Nevertheless, economic stratum were still present at this time.

Item 12.
A.   Many of the warriors invading had established themselves as affluent farmers.
B.   Many of the warriors had established themselves invading as affluent farmers.
C.   Many of the invading warriors had established themselves as affluent farmers.
D.   Invading many of the warriors had established themselves as affluent farmers.

Item 13.

    A.   It's wealth was in stark contrast to the life of the lower class slaves and peasants,

    B.   Its wealth was in stark contrast to the life of the lower class slaves and peasants,

    C.   Their wealth was in stark contrast to the life of the lower class slaves and peasants,

    D.   The wealth of their's was in stark contrast to the life of the lower class slaves and peasants,

Item 14.

    A.   who often had large families.

    B.   who often lived with their families.

    C.   who often lived in extremely poor conditions.

    D.   who were often born and working in the countryside.

Item 15.

    A.   In addition, this period witnessed the rise in imperialism, defined as a political system for which a king or queen has absolute power.

    B.   In addition, this period witnessed the rise in imperialism, defined as a political system in which a king or queen has absolute power.

    C.   In addition, this period witnessed the rise in imperialism, defined as a political system which a king or queen has absolute power.

    D.   In addition, this period witnessed the rise in imperialism, defined as a political system, which a king or queen has absolute power.

Item 16.

    A.   While many kings strived to rule in accordance with the law, some rulers treated their citizens harshly, without establishing followed legal restrictions.

    B.   While many kings strived to rule in accordance with the law, some rulers treated their citizens harshly, without followed establishing legal restrictions.

    C.   While many kings strived to rule in accordance with the law, some rulers treated their citizens harshly, without following established legal restrictions.

    D.   While many kings strived to rule in accordance with the law, some rulers treated their citizens harshly, without legal following established restrictions.

Item 17.

    A.   Yet, their appalling living conditions, the common populace began to challenge the imperial system during the Middle Ages.

    B.   Yet, in spite their appalling living conditions, the common populace began to challenge the imperial system during the Middle Ages.

    C.   Yet, despite their appalling living conditions, the common populace began to challenge the imperial system during the Middle Ages.

    D.   Yet, although their appalling living conditions, the common populace began to challenge the imperial system during the Middle Ages.

Item 18.

    A.   Changing the attitudes of people towards their rulers,

    B.   As changing as the attitudes of people towards their rulers,

    C.   As the attitudes of people towards their rulers changed,

    D.   As changed the attitudes of people towards their rulers,

Item 19.

    A.   the balance of power in the political system also began to have shift.

    B.   the balance of power in the political system also began to had shift.

    C.   the balance of power in the political system also began to have shifted.

    D.   the balance of power in the political system also began to shift.

Item 20.

    A.   To a significant extent, these challenges influenced the functioning of present-day political systems.

    B.   To a significant extent these challenges, influenced the functioning of present-day political systems.

    C.   To a significant extent these challenges influenced, the functioning of present-day political systems.

    D.   To a significant extent these challenges influenced the functioning, of present-day political systems.

Item 21.

Suppose the purpose of this assignment was to explain how the Middle Ages affected current political systems. Has the student achieved this purpose?

- A. No, because the student has not given a detailed explanation of the functioning of modern-day political systems.
- B. No, because the student has not sufficiently related aspects of the Middle Age system to current politics.
- C. Yes, because the student has mentioned the effect of the Middle Ages on present-day democracy, as well as its relationship with multi-ethnicity.
- D. Yes, because the student has enumerated similarities between aspects of the Roman government with those of the present day.

ANSWERS TO THE ESSAY CORRECTION EXERCISES

ESSAY 1

1) D

2) A

3) D

4) C

5) B

6) A

7) B

8) C

9) C

10) C

11) D

12) D

13) B

14) C

15) B

16) C

17) A

18) D

19) B

20) B

21) D

22) A

ESSAY 2

1) B

2) C

3) D

4) C

5) D

6) D

7) D

8) C

9) C

10) B

11) B

12) C

13) C

14) C

15) B

16) C

17) C

18) C

19) D

20) A

21) B

Made in United States
Orlando, FL
12 April 2023

32035345R00080